Cooking with Larry

A Collection of Favorites

Larry Brandenburg

Cooking with Larry
Copyright © 2025 Larry Brandenburg
Published by Kingdom Publishing Press
Franklin, Tennessee, USA

All rights reserved. No part of this publication may be reproduced, digitally stored, or transmitted in any form without the permission of Kingdom Publishing Press.

ISBN: 979-8-9933640-1-8

Printed in the United States of America

Cooking with Larry

A Collection of Favorites

"If more of us valued food and cheer and song above hoarded gold, it would be a merrier world."

— J.R.R. Tolkien

The Hobbit

Forward

"Made this recipe on Oct 18, 2019 and turned out good. Red pepper in original recipe was too much so I removed it." – Larry Brandenburg

Ecclesiastes 1:9 says, "What has been, it is what will be, and what has been done, it is what will be done. So there is nothing new under the sun." This book of recipes is "nothing new under the sun", but rather a collection of Larry's favorites, gathered from family, friends, friends of friends, cookbooks, online resources, and Larry's own creations—formulated from his gift of culinary inquisitiveness.

We may never know the origin of many of these recipes, some only providing a name, a piece of history, or a link to an internet presence. And while it is possible to investigate a bit deeper into the singular source in order to properly give credit where credit is due, the truth is, there is no way of knowing if any of these recipes are in their original form, as Larry had a unique way of making each recipe his very own, leaving his mark on everything he created, adding a teaspoon here or substituting there.

Many of these recipes were family favorites, familiar tastes and smells in the House of Brandenburg. They became our traditions, our expectations at family gatherings, along with the story of their history or a recollection of the inspiration.

Larry fed us physically and spiritually, pouring into us through his knowledge and his gifts. We were so blessed to have such a man in our lives, a man who loved the Lord and his family well. I hope that all who stumble upon this collection of favorites will find joy in the familiarity of those they remember and the novelty of those he finely tuned, seeing the husband, father, father-in-law, grandfather, and friend, as they embark on a journey while *Cooking with Larry*.

Table of Contents

> ### *Momma's Something*
>
> 1 1/2 cup warm water
> 1 packet yeast
> 2 tablespoons Lard
> 1 tsp salt
> 1 egg beaten
> 2 tbs
> 4 cups flour

Breads

Best Biscuits Yet	1
Buttermilk Biscuits	2
Yeast Rolls	3
Yeast Rolls – 2	4

Desserts

3-Minute No-Bake Cookies	7
6 in. Cheesecake – Larry's New York Style	8
Amazing Pie	9
Amazing Strawberry Pound Cake	10

Apple Fritter Cake	11
Apple Fritter Cake – 2	13
Aunt Reba's Lemon Cake	15
Banana Cream Pie	16
Banana Split Pie	17
Best Ever Sticky Buns (No Machine)	18
Bread Pudding	21
Butter Cream Icing	22
Butternuts Cookies	23
Butterscotch Cake	24
Carrot Cake	26
Carrot Cake Roll	27
Chocolate Oatmeal No Bake Cookies	29
Christmas Snowball Cookies	29
Cinnabon Cake	30
Cinnamon Sticky Buns Recipe	31
Coca-Cola Cake Recipe	33
Cream Cheese Icing	34
Crust	35
Easy Chocolate Cake	39
Coconut Cream Pie	41
German's Chocolate Cake	42
Gigi's Coconut Pie	44
Gigi's Crust	44
Great Grandma's Coconut Cream Pie	45
Harvest Cinnamon Rolls Recipe – Perfect Cinnamon Rolls	46
Helen Huff Butterscotch Pie	48
Hershey Brownies	49
Hershey's Chocolate Cake	51
Granny's Old Fashioned Bread Pudding with Vanilla Sauce	53
Ingredients (for cake)	54
Kentucky Butter Poke Cake	55

Lindy's Cheesecake	57
Melt in Your Mouth Strawberry Pound Cake	59
Milky Way Cake	60
Momma's Boiled Custard	61
Most Amazing Chocolate Cake	62
Old Fashion Pie	64
Old Fashion Bread Pudding	65
Old Fashion Bread Pudding – 2	66
Old Fashion Custard Pie	67
Orange Dream-sicle Cake	68
Pate Brisee Recipe	70
Payday Bars	72
Peach Cobbler	73
Pound Cake	74
Pistachio Delight	74
Raspberry Cream Cheese Sweet Rolls	75
Raspberry Zinger Poke Cake	78
Sandy Apple Crisp	79
Shirley Temple Cake (Larry Version)	81
Snickerdoodles	83
Surprise Carrot Cake	84
Ten Minute Pie Crust	85
Toasted Coconut Tres Leches Pound Cake	86
Twinkies Recipe	87
Vanilla Roll Cake	89
Vickie Crowley Butterscotch Pie	90
Whipped Cream Cheese	92
Yellow Cake	93
Zucchini Banana Cake	94

Dishes and Dough

Baked Burrito Casserole	97
Chicken Broccoli Stir Fry	98
Deep Dish Pizza	100
Gumbo	104
Old Fashioned Chicken and Dumplings	105
Papas Shrimp and Grits	107
Pizza Dough	108
Weeknight Bolognese	109

Dressings and Dips

Buffalo Chicken Dip	113
Southern Slaw Dressing	114

Meats

Mongolian Beef	117
Peppered Beef with Onion	118
Perfect Prime Rib	119
Slow Cooked Salisbury Steak	121

Salsa, Sauces, Seasonings, and Sides

Bill Knapp's Coleslaw	125
Cajun Cream Sauce	126
Cajun Seasoning	126
Cucumber Sauce	127
Italian Seasoning	128
Peach Salsa	128
Peanut Sauce	129
Red Lobster Tartar Sauce	130
Tartar Sauce – Red Lobster Style	131

Soups

Larry's Corn Chowder	135
Larry's Corn Chowder – 2	136
Potato Chowder	137
Red Beans and Rice	138
Red Beans and Rice Recipe	139
Shrimp and Crab Bisque	141
Slow Cooker Creamy Tortellini Soup	143

Breads

Best Biscuits Yet

2 cups all-purpose bread flour (King Arthur)
2 1/2 tsp baking powder
1 tsp salt
1/3 cup Crisco
1 cup whole milk

In a bowl, mix flour baking powder and salt, stir with a whisk until smooth.

Add Crisco and cut in with a Pastry cutter until small pea size. Add milk and work into a ball. Turn out on a floured surface and knead until smooth. Use a roller to roll into a 3/4-inch thickness. I use a glass to cut out biscuits (should make 8 to 10). I use a greased black iron skillet. Place biscuits close together and place in a 425 pre-heated oven for 18-22 minutes until golden brown. Brush with butter and serve.

I use this recipe for dumplings also. Reduce baking powder to 1 tsp and roll down to 1/4 inch then cut into 1 x 2-inch rectangles. Boil in chicken broth until firm. Add chicken and 1 can of cream of chicken soup + 1/2 cup whole milk.

Buttermilk Biscuits

December 12, 2015, 2:07 PM

2 ½ cups of self-rising flour (I use White Lily)
¼ cup of cold Crisco
¼ cup of cold butter
Buttermilk

Cut the fats into the flour until the size of peas. I don't measure my liquid; I just add buttermilk until I have a very wet (?) sticky. Roll out onto a heavy floured surface. Flatten the dough to form a rectangle about 5" x 10 inches I then take a large spatula and lift up each end and fold it over to the center (?). Do this four times. The folding creates layers. Add more flour as needed. Finally pat down to about 1 inch thick. Then take your biscuit cutter and do not* twist. Twisting seals the edges and they don't rise as good. Place them in a while greased round 8 x 8 pan with the edges touching. I always squeeze two into the center. It makes them a little thicker. Bake at 425° about 15 to 20 minutes or until golden brown.

*"do not" added in editing as a portion of this recipe was missing.

Yeast Rolls

1 pkg active dry yeast (equals 2 1/4 tsp)
1/4 c warm water
1/3 c white, granulated sugar
1/4 c butter, softened
1 tsp salt
1 c hot milk
1 egg, lightly beaten
4 1/2 c sifted all-purpose flour
2 Tbsp butter, melted (for brushing rolls)

Sprinkle yeast over very warm water in large bowl. Stir until yeast dissolves. Add sugar, the 1/4 cup butter and salt to hot milk and stir until sugar dissolves and butter is melted. Cool mixture to 105 to 115 degrees. Leave to foam about 10 minutes.

Add milk mixture to yeast and then mix in egg. Beat in 4 cups of the flour, 1 cup at a time, to form a soft dough. Use some of remaining 1/2 cup flour to dust a pastry cloth.

Knead the dough lightly for 5 minutes. Use remaining flour for flouring pastry cloth and your hands.

Place dough in a warm, buttered bowl; turn greased side up. Cover and let rise in warm place until doubled in bulk, about 1 1/4 to 1 1/2 hours.

Punch dough down and knead 4 to 5 minutes on a lightly floured pastry cloth. Dough will be sticky but use as little flour as possible for flouring hands, otherwise rolls will not be as feathery light as they should be.

With large knife, cut dough ball into four (4) pieces. Cut each piece into four (4) more pieces OR simply pinch off small chunks of dough and roll into round balls about 1 3/4 inches in diameter. As you roll into balls, pull sides down and under to shape roll. Place bottom side down in neat rows, not quite touching, in well-buttered 13 X 9 X 2-inch pan.

Cover rolls and allow to rise in warm place until doubled in bulk; 30 - 45 minutes. When doubled in bulk, brush tops with melted butter and bake in 375-degree F oven for 18 - 20 minutes or until nicely browned. My oven runs hot so I usually bake @ 325 so tops do not brown before rolls are done inside. Adjust your oven temp accordingly.

If desired, brush (or bathe!) rolls in more melted butter when they are hot. The butter will sizzle down sides and bottom of rolls for a buttery soft crust.

Yeast Rolls -2

1 c water, warm
1 pkg active dry yeast
1/4 c sugar
1 tsp salt
3 Tbsp butter, softened
1 large egg, beaten
3 1/2 - 4 c all-purpose flour

Desserts

3-Minute No-Bake Cookies

2 cups granulated sugar
8 tablespoons (1 stick) margarine or butter
1/2 cup low-fat milk
1/4 cup baking cocoa
1 cup Smooth Peanut Butter
1/4 salt
1 tsp vanilla extract
3 cups Quaker® Oats (quick or old fashioned, uncooked)

In large saucepan, combine sugar, margarine, milk and cocoa. Bring to boil over medium heat, stirring frequently. Continue boiling 3 minutes, stirring frequently. Remove from heat. Stir in oats, salt, peanut butter and vanilla extract. Drop by tablespoonfuls onto waxed paper. Makes about 3 dozen. Let stand until firm. Store tightly covered.

Serving Tips: *If using old fashioned oats, cool mixture in saucepan 5 minutes.

6 in. Cheesecake - Larry's New York Style

2 blocks 8 oz Philly cream softened
½ cup sugar
½ cup sour cream
1 ½ tbs flour
2 eggs
1 tbs vanilla

Crust
3/4 cup graham cracker crumbs
3 tbs sugar
3 tbs butter

Crust
Melt butter and mix with graham cracker and sugar in a bowl. Pat into bottom of a lined 6-inch pie pan. Bake for 15 minutes set aside and cool to room temperature.

Cake
In a mixing bowl, mix cream cheese, sour cream, sugar, flour and vanilla. Blend until lumps are gone. Mix in eggs one at a time until blended. Pour into greased spring form pan and replace in a water bath (line bottom of pan with aluminum foil to make watertight). Bake 45 minutes and turn oven off. Open door and let cool for two hours (this will help cake not to split). Slide a knife blade around edge to separate from pan. Chill in refrigerator and serve.

Amazing Pie

2 cups milk
3/4 cups sugar
1/2 cup Bisquick
4 eggs
1/4 cup butter
1 1/2 tbs vanilla
Optional
1 1/3 cups coconut

Combine all ingredients except coconut in a blender and blend for three minutes on low speed. Pour into a greased pie pan and let set for five minutes.

Sprinkle on coconut if using and bake at 350 for 40 minutes until golden brown

For custard pie omit coconut and sprinkle on ground nutmeg

Amazing Strawberry Pound Cake

"This is technically considered half pound cake because it calls for half the amount of sugar, flour and butter. But amazing still."

1 cup butter
1 1/2 cups white sugar
2 eggs
1 teaspoon vanilla extract
1 teaspoon ground almonds
2 cups all-purpose flour
1/3 cup milk
1 cup quartered strawberries
1/4 cup water

Preheat oven to 350 degrees F (175 degrees C). Grease 2 loaf pans or 1 square baking dish.

Beat butter and sugar with an electric mixer in a large bowl until light and fluffy. The mixture should be noticeably lighter in color. Add eggs one at a time, allowing each egg to blend into the butter mixture before adding the next. Beat in vanilla extract and ground almonds with the last egg. Pour flour alternately with milk, mixing until just incorporated. Fold in strawberries and water; mixing just enough to evenly combine. Pour the batter into prepared pans.

Bake in the preheated oven until a toothpick inserted into the center comes out clean, about 1 hour. Run a paring knife between the cake and the edge of the pans and allow cake to cool completely before removing.

Apple Fritter Cake

For Filling:
1 heaping cup of sliced apples (I cored and quartered and then sliced)
1/3 cup sugar
1/4 teaspoon cinnamon
Small pinch freshly grated nutmeg
2 tablespoons cornstarch
2 teaspoons water
Plus
1/2 cup brown sugar (I used a 1/4 cup each of dark and light)
1/2 teaspoon cinnamon

For Cake:
1/3 cup butter
3/4 cup sugar
1/2 cup applesauce
1 teaspoon vanilla
2 eggs
2 1/4 cups flour
1 teaspoon baking powder
1 teaspoon baking soda
1 teaspoon salt
1 teaspoon cinnamon
1 cup Greek yogurt (you could use plain yogurt as well or sour cream)

For Glaze:
1 cup powdered sugar
1 teaspoon vanilla
6 tablespoons milk

For Filling: Make your filling by combining apples, sugar, water, cinnamon and cornstarch in a small saucepan. Cook on low heat for 5 to 7 minutes, stirring constantly until the sauce is thickened and the apples are a bit soft. Set aside to cool. In a small bowl, mix the brown sugar and cinnamon together until well combined and set aside.

For Cake: Preheat oven to 350°. Grease and flour a 9×13 baking dish. Set aside.

Cream butter and sugar until light and fluffy, about 3 minutes. Add applesauce and vanilla and mix till combined. Add the eggs, one at a time, beating well after each addition.

Sift the dry ingredients together. Add the dry ingredients to the batter in three parts alternating with the yogurt in two parts, beginning and ending with the dry ingredients. Beat until just combined.

Spoon half of the batter into the prepared pan. Spoon the cooled apple mixture over the batter carefully and spread as evenly as possible. Sprinkle 2/3 of brown sugar cinnamon mixture over apples and cover with the rest of the batter. Sprinkle the rest of the brown sugar cinnamon mixture over the top.

Bake for 45-55 minutes, until a toothpick inserted into the center of the cake comes out clean.

For Glaze: While the cake is baking, make the glaze. In a bowl, mix the powdered sugar, vanilla, and milk until the glaze is desired consistency. When the cake comes out of the oven, immediately but carefully pour onto hot cake. Try to pour as evenly as possible. You might have to pick up the cake and tilt it to spread the glaze evenly. I even poured some out that pooled at the corners and repoured that over the top. Let the cake sit for a while for the glaze to set.

Apple Fritter Cake – 2

For Filling:
1 heaping cup of sliced apples (I cored and quartered and then sliced)
1/3 cup sugar
1/4 teaspoon cinnamon
Small pinch freshly grated nutmeg
1 tablespoons cornstarch
2 teaspoons water
Plus
1/2 cup brown sugar (I used a 1/4 cup each of dark and light)
1/2 teaspoon cinnamon

For Cake:
1/3 cup butter
3/4 cup sugar
1/2 cup applesauce
1 teaspoon vanilla
1 egg
2 1/4 cups flour
1 teaspoon baking powder
1 teaspoon baking soda
1 teaspoon salt
1 teaspoon cinnamon
1 cup Greek yogurt (you could use plain yogurt as well or sour cream)

For Glaze:
2 cups powdered sugar
1 teaspoon vanilla
6 tablespoons mild

For Filling: Make your filling by combining apples, sugar, water, cinnamon and cornstarch in a small saucepan. Cook on low heat for 5 to 7 minutes, stirring constantly until the sauce is thickened and the apples are a bit soft. Set aside to cool. In a small bowl, mix the brown sugar and cinnamon together until well combined and set aside.

For Cake: Preheat oven to 350°. Grease and flour a 9×13 baking dish. Set aside.

Cream butter and sugar until light and fluffy, about 3 minutes. Add applesauce and vanilla and mix till combined. Add the eggs, one at a time, beating well after each addition.

Sift the dry ingredients together. Add the dry ingredients to the batter in three parts alternating with the yogurt in two parts, beginning and ending with the dry ingredients. Beat until just combined.

Spoon half of the batter into the prepared pan. Spoon the cooled apple mixture over the batter carefully and spread as evenly as possible. Sprinkle 2/3 of brown sugar cinnamon mixture over apples and cover with the rest of the batter. Sprinkle the rest of the brown sugar cinnamon mixture over the top.

Bake for 45-55 minutes, until a toothpick inserted into the center of the cake comes out clean.

For Glaze: While the cake is baking, make the glaze. In a bowl, mix the powdered sugar, vanilla, and milk until the glaze is desired consistency. When the cake comes out of the oven, immediately but carefully pour onto hot cake. Try to pour as evenly as possible. You might have to pick up the cake and tilt it to spread the glaze evenly. I even poured some out that pooled at the corners and repoured that over the top. Let the cake sit for a while for the glaze to set

Aunt Reba's Lemon Cake

1 box yellow cake mix (Betty Crocker)
1 small instant Lemon pudding mix
3/4 cup oil
3/4 cup milk
5 large eggs
2 tsps vanilla

Mix well and pour into a greased cake pan. Bake at 350 for 45 minutes. Cool and invert onto a cake plate.

Sauce
1/3 cup orange juice
2 tbs lemon juice
2 cups powdered sugar

Make hole in cooled cake and pour sauce over. Put back into oven for 5 minutes.

Banana Cream Pie

1 (9 inch) pie crusts, baked
3 cups whole milk
3/4 cup white sugar
1/3 cup all-purpose flour
1/4 teaspoon salt
3 egg yolks, slightly beaten
2 tablespoons butter
1 teaspoon vanilla
3 bananas

Have baked 9-inch pie shell ready.

In a large saucepan, scald the milk. In another saucepan, combine the sugar, flour and salt; gradually stir in the scalded milk. Over medium heat, stirring constantly, cook until thickened. Cover and, stirring occasionally, cook for two minutes longer.

In a small bowl, have the 3 egg yolks, slightly beaten, ready; stir a small amount of the hot mixture into beaten yolks; when thoroughly combined, stir yolks into hot mixture. Cook for one minute longer, stirring constantly. Remove from heat and blend in the butter and vanilla. Let sit until lukewarm.

When ready to pour, slice bananas and scatter in pie shell; pour warm mixture over bananas.

If desired, make a meringue (you'll have 3 leftover egg whites) to top the pie, or just let the pie cool until serving.

Banana Split Pie

1 stick butter, melted
1 box graham cracker crumbs
1 stick butter, softened
2 eggs
2 cups confectioners' sugar
5 bananas, sliced
1 (15 ounces) can crush pineapple, undrained
1 (16 ounces) container Cool-Whip, thawed
1 (4 ounces) jar maraschino cherries, stemmed
½ cup pecans, chopped
Chocolate Syrup, Optional

In a 9×13 glass or porcelain dish, combine 1 stick of melted butter and graham cracker crumbs. With a fork, incorporate the butter until the crumbs are coated. Firmly press into a crust in the bottom of the pan.

In a medium bowl, cream together the other stick of softened butter, eggs and confectioners' sugar; beat for 15 minutes. Spread evenly on the graham cracker crust. Layer banana slices evenly on top of butter/sugar mixture; layer pineapple on top of the bananas. Evenly spread the Cool-Whip and garnish with cherries and pecans. Drizzle optional chocolate syrup over the top. Refrigerate at least 2 hours or overnight. Keeps well refrigerated for about a week.

Note: We prefer this without the chocolate syrup

Best Ever Sticky Buns (No Machine)

Prep Time 30 mins
Cook Time 40 mins
Total Time 1 hr 10 mins

Make my soft, caramel and pecan Best Ever Sticky Buns without a mixer and no-kneading required!

Course: Dessert
Cuisine: American
Servings: 8

1 cups (8oz / 240g) milk
2 teaspoons Fast acting dried yeast or Instant yeast
2 teaspoons salt
2 large eggs, lightly beaten
¼ cup (2 ½ oz/75g) honey
½ cup (4oz/115g) butter, melted
3 ½ cups (18½ oz/525g) all-purpose flour

Caramel Topping and Filling
¾ cup (6oz/170g) butter, melted, plus more for sides of the pan
1 ¼ cup (7 ½ oz/220g) brown sugar
⅓ cup (4oz/115g) honey
1 teaspoon ground cinnamon
½ teaspoon salt
1 ½ cups (4 ½ oz/105g) chopped pecans

In a large bowl combine the flour, yeast and salt. Set aside.

In a separate jug, mix together the milk, honey, butter. Pop in the microwave and gently heat for a few seconds until the mix is lukewarm and the butter is melting.

Once the butter has melted quickly whisk in the eggs until combined. You want to make sure the mix isn't hot otherwise the eggs will cook.

Pour the wet into the dry and mix until it forms a dough and all the flour is mixed in. It only takes a minutes to mix the dough together.

Cover with cling wrap and allow to rest at room temperature until the dough rises for a minimum of 4 hours. After the 4 hours you can place it in the fridge for up to 4 days.

For the Filling: Mix together melted butter, brown sugar, honey and cinnamon. Set aside.

Using a 9-inch cake pan, with a spatula spread half the caramel mixture evenly over the bottom and all over the sides. Scatter the pecans over the caramel mixture and set aside.

Dust your work surface with flour. Roll out the dough to a 1/8-inch-thick rectangle (around 20 inches long). As you roll out the dough, make sure there is enough flour to prevent it from sticking to the work surface.

With the remaining caramel mixture evenly spread it over the rolled out dough leaving 1 inch around the edge of the dough without the filling.

Starting with the long side, roll the dough into a log. Roll it over until its seam is underneath.

Using a serrated knife, cut the log into 2 ½ inch rolls (around 8/9 pieces). Arrange the rolls over the pecans in the prepared pan, so that the swirled cut edge is facing upward.

Cover the tin with plastic wrap and allow to rest for 1 hour. During this time they will rise up to meet the tin and becoming bubbly.

Once proofed, place the rolls on a baking sheet covered with parchment, in case the caramel bubbles over.

Preheat the oven to 350oF (180oC) and bake for roughly 40 minutes, or until golden brown and firm in the center.

While still hot, run a thin spatula around the outer edge of the pan to release the caramel rolls, and invert immediately onto a serving dish. If you let them set too long, they will stick to the pan and will be difficult to turn out. Enjoy warm!

Bread Pudding

2 cups milk
1/4 cup butter
1/2 cup sugar
2 eggs, slightly beaten
1 tablespoon vanilla
1/2 teaspoon ground nutmeg

Sauce
1/2 cup butter
1/2 cup sugar
1/2 cup firmly packed brown sugar
1/2 cup heavy whipping cream
1 tablespoon vanilla

For the Pudding: Heat oven to 350°F. Combine bread and raisins in large bowl. Combine milk and 1/4 cup butter in 1-quart saucepan. Cook over medium heat until butter is melted (4 to 7 minutes). Pour milk mixture over bread; let stand 10 minutes.

Stir in all remaining pudding ingredients. Pour into greased 1 1/2-quart casserole. Bake for 40 to 50 minutes or until set in center.

For the Sauce: Combine all sauce ingredients except vanilla in 1-quart saucepan. Cook over medium heat, stirring occasionally, until mixture thickens and comes to a full boil (5 to 8 minutes). Stir in vanilla.

To serve, spoon warm pudding into individual dessert dishes; serve with sauce. Store refrigerated. OR

Butter Cream Icing

3 sticks unsalted butter, softened
Tiny pinch fine sea salt
1 ½ pounds (24 ounces) powdered sugar, sifted
1 tablespoon clear vanilla extract (this helps maintain the bright white color)
2-3 tablespoons heavy cream or milk

In the bowl of a stand mixer fitted with the paddle attachment, beat the butter on medium-high speed for 6-7 minutes.

With the mixer on low speed, slowly add in the salt and powdered sugar, and continue beating until the sugar is fully incorporated.

Add in vanilla and cream or milk and mix on low speed until incorporated. Turn the mixer back up to medium-high speed and beat the buttercream for an additional 6-7 minutes.

If the buttercream is too thick, add in a bit of milk, one teaspoon at a time until you reach the desired consistency.

Butternuts Cookies
(Added by Denise Hagar)

"These are my most requested cookie. I usually make at least 500 of these at Christmas. It's a very simple recipe but packed with lots a flavor!"

Cook Time: 15 Min
Prep Time: 5 Min
Serves: 3 dozen

3/4 c butter, room temperature + 1 Tbsp.
1/2 c powdered sugar
1/4 tsp salt
1 3/4 c all-purpose flour
6 oz package butterscotch chips
1 c finely chopped pecans

Rum Glaze
3 c powdered sugar
1 tsp rum extract
1/2 c chopped pecans
3 to 4 Tbsp milk or water

Cream butter with powdered sugar and salt til light and fluffy. Blend in flour, mix well. Add butterscotch chips and 1 cup finely chopped pecans. Shape dough, a scant teaspoonful at a time, into balls. Place 1 inch apart on ungreased cookie sheet. Bake in 325 degree oven for 15 minutes or until firm but not brown. Let cool on wire racks. Make rum glaze. Mix the ingredients until smooth. You can either dip the cookies in the glaze or use a spoon to pour over cookies. Sprinkle with chopped pecans.

Last Step: Don't forget to share! Make all your friends drool by posting a picture of your finished recipe on your favorite social network. And don't forget to tag Just A Pinch and include #justapinchrecipes so we can see it too!

Butterscotch Cake

2 cups Brown Sugar
1/2 cup Butter
1 teaspoon vanilla
2 eggs
2 cups Flour
1 teaspoon Baking Soda
1 teaspoon Baking Powder
1/2 teaspoon salt
1 cup Buttermilk

Preheat oven to 350 degrees. Grease and flour (or line with parchment) two 9" or three 6" round pans.

Cream the butter and sugar with an electric mixer on medium until fluffy. Add vanilla, then add eggs one at a time, beating on low just until they are mixed in.

In a separate bowl, sift together the flour, baking soda, baking powder and salt. Starting with the flour mixture, add the flour and the buttermilk (alternating one then the other) into the sugar/egg mixture on low speed. When everything is mixed in, scrape down the bowl by hand.

Pour batter into the pans and bake for 25-30 minutes, until a toothpick inserted in the middle comes out clean. Cool before frosting.

Caramel Icing
1 1/2 cups Brown Sugar
1 Tablespoon flour
1/4 Cup butter (plus 2 tablespoons for later)
1/4 Cup Milk
1 teaspoon vanilla

In a small saucepan, mix together all ingredients except the vanilla and the extra 2 Tablespoons of butter. Heat over medium and bring to a boil. Stirring frequently to prevent burning, let the mixture boil for a good one minute. (I actually use a candy thermometer and let it reach 238 degrees, but if you don't have one, just make sure you boil it for a good solid minute).

Butterscotch Cake Caramel Icing
Take off the fire and add in the vanilla and the 2 Tablespoons butter. Cool the mixture, occasionally giving it a vigorous stir, until it is still warm (but not HOT) and has thickened enough to spread. Spread it over the cake, moving fairly quickly because it will set as it cools. It will be a thin coating, not a thick layer. Let it set completely before cutting into the cake.

Carrot Cake

2 cups sugar
3/4 cup vegetable oil
3 eggs
1 1/4 cups Daisy Sour Cream
3 teaspoons vanilla
2 1/2 cups all purpose flour
2 teaspoons baking soda
2 teaspoons cinnamon
1/2 teaspoon salt
1/4 teaspoon ground nutmeg
3 cups shredded carrots
1 cup chopped pecans
4 1/2 cups powdered sugar
1/3 cup butter, softened

Heat the oven to 350 degrees. Grease and flour 3 (8-inch) round cake pans. In large bowl, beat the sugar, oil and eggs until creamy. Add ¾ cup sour cream and 2 teaspoons vanilla; beat until well-mixed. Add flour, baking soda, cinnamon, salt, and nutmeg. Beat on low speed until mixed. Beat on medium speed for 1 minute. Stir in the carrots and nuts. Pour the batter evenly into the pans. Bake for 20 to 30 minutes or until toothpick inserted in center comes out clean. Cool in the pans for 10 minutes. Remove the cakes from pans onto cooling racks; cool completely, about 1 hour. In a medium bowl, combine powdered sugar, 1/3 cup softened butter, 1/2 cup sour cream, and 1 teaspoon vanilla; beat on low speed until mixed. Beat on medium speed until smooth and creamy. Place 1 cake layer, rounded side down, on a serving plate. Tuck strips of waxed paper under bottom edge of cake all around cake. Spread about 1/2 cup frosting over cake. Place second layer over frosting, rounded side up. Repeat with third layer. Frost the sides and top of the cake. Remove the strips of waxed paper. Store covered in refrigerator.

Carrot Cake Roll

Cake
3/4 cup flour
2 tsp. ground cinnamon
1 tsp. baking powder
1/2 tsp. kosher salt
1/2 tsp. ground ginger
1/4 tsp. ground nutmeg
1/8 tsp. ground cloves
3 large eggs
1/2 cup granulated sugar
2 tbsp. vegetable oil
1 tsp. pure vanilla extract
3 medium carrots, shredded

Filling
1 cup confectioners' sugar
1 (8 oz.) package cream cheese, softened
6 tbsp. salted butter, softened
1 tsp. pure vanilla extract

Glaze Drizzle
3 cups confectioners' sugar
1/2 teaspoon vanilla extract
10-11 tbsp. milk

Preheat oven to 375 degrees F and line a 15 x 10-inch jelly roll pan with parchment paper, leaving a little overhang on each side.

In a medium bowl, combine flour, cinnamon, baking powder, salt, ginger, nutmeg, and cloves and whisk.

In a large bowl, combine eggs and sugar and whisk until combined.

Add vegetable oil, vanilla extract, and carrots and mix again until combined.

Pour the dry ingredients into the large bowl and fold to combine.

Stir batter just until combined. Pour batter into the jelly roll pan and spread into an even layer. Bake for 12 minutes and remove the cake from the pan using the overhang on the sides.

Lay cake on a large wood cutting board and gently roll the cake lengthwise. Carefully transfer the cake to a cooling rack and let cool completely.

For the Filling: Combine confectioners' sugar, cream cheese, butter, and vanilla extract in a medium bowl and whisk until smooth and creamy.

Carefully unroll the cake and spread the filling onto the cake, allowing for a small gap on all edges.

Reroll the cake and wrap it tightly with plastic cling wrap.
Chill in the fridge for 1 hour before serving.

When ready to serve, combine the glaze ingredients in a mixing bowl and whisk until smooth. Drizzle over the cake and slice.

ENJOY!

Chocolate Oatmeal No Bake Cookies

1/2 c Butter
2 c Sugar
1/2 c Milk
4 Tbsp Cocoa
1/2 c Peanut Butter
3 1/2 c Quick cooking Oats
2 tsp. Vanilla

Add the first 4 ingredients in a saucepan. Bring to a rolling boil and boil for 1 minute. Stir in the next 3 ingredients and drop onto wax/foil paper. Let cool until set.

Christmas Snowball Cookies

1cup butter, softened
1/2 cup powdered sugar
1teaspoons vanilla
2 cups all-purpose flour
1/4 teaspoon salt
1 cup pecans, chopped powdered sugar

Blend softened butter with powdered sugar. Add vanilla. Mix in salt, flour and chopped pecans. Form dough into 1-inch balls or flattened cookies and place on an ungreased cookie sheet. Bake in a 325-degree oven for 20 minutes. While hot, roll in powdered sugar. Let cool and roll again in powdered sugar.

Cinnabon Cake

3 cups flour
1/4 teaspoon salt
1 cup sugar
4 teaspoons baking powder
1 1/2 cups milk
2 eggs
2 teaspoons vanilla
½ cup butter, melted

Topping
1 cup butter, softened
1 cup brown sugar
1 tablespoon flour
1 tablespoon cinnamon

Glaze
2 cups powdered sugar
5 tablespoons milk
1 teaspoon vanilla

Preheat oven to 350F. Prepare a 9 x 13 baking pan (buttered). Mix all of the base ingredients together, with the exception of the butter. Add the melted butter last and then pour into your prepared pan. Mix all of the topping ingredients together in a separate bowl. Mix well. Drop by teaspoonful over the base, as evenly as you can over the entire base. Take a butter knife and swirl the topping into the base. Pop into the oven and bake for 28-30 minutes.

While the cake is baking, prepare the glaze and set aside. Remove from oven and glaze the cake while still warm.

Cinnamon Sticky Buns Recipe

Dough
1/4 cup warm water (105° to 115°)
1 (1/4-ounce) package active dry yeast
1/3 cup sugar
3/4 cup milk
4 Tbsp. unsalted butter, plus more for greasing
3 large egg yolks
1 Tbsp. finely grated orange zest
1 1/4 teaspoon. salt
4 to 4 1/4 cups all-purpose flour, plus more for dusting

Filling
1/2 cup firmly packed light brown sugar
1 Tbsp. ground cinnamon
4 Tbsp. unsalted butter

Topping
3/4 cup firmly packed light brown sugar
4 Tbsp. unsalted butter
3 Tbsp. honey
1 Tbsp. light corn syrup
1 1/2 cups (6 ounces) coarsely chopped pecans

Method
Make the dough. In the bowl of an electric mixer, combine warm water, yeast and 1 tsp. sugar. Stir to dissolve and let sit until foamy, about 5 minutes.

Add milk, butter, remaining sugar, egg yolks, orange zest, salt and 3 cups flour. Mix on low speed until blended. Switch to a dough hook and then, again on low speed, slowly incorporate the remaining 1 cup of flour. Increase speed to medium, kneading dough until smooth and slightly sticky (adding a little more flour if too wet), 3 to 5 minutes. Shape the dough into a ball and place in a large, buttered bowl. Turn dough over in bowl to coat with the butter from the bowl. Cover the bowl with plastic wrap. Let rise in a warm place until doubled in volume, about 1 hour (or 2 hours if not in an entirely warm place). After the dough has risen, punch down. Turn out onto a lightly floured cutting board and let sit 20 minutes.

Make the filling. Combine brown sugar and cinnamon in a small bowl. Melt butter; keep separate.

Roll dough out into a 12" x 18" rectangle. Brush with melted butter and sprinkle with cinnamon-sugar mixture. Starting with the long side, roll dough into a cylinder. Place seam side down on a flat surface and cut crosswise into 15 slices.

Make the topping. In a 1-quart saucepan, combine brown sugar, butter, honey and corn syrup over low heat; stir until sugar and butter are melted. Pour mixture into a greased 9" x 13" pan and sprinkle pecans on top.

Place dough slices, flat side down, on top of prepared topping. Crowd them so they touch. Cover with plastic wrap, leaving room for the buns to rise, and refrigerate overnight.

Remove the rolls from the refrigerator and let stand at room temperature while the oven pre-heats. Preheat oven to 375°. Bake buns until golden, 30 to 35 minutes. Remove pan from oven and immediately (and carefully as not to spill hot topping on your toes!) invert onto a serving tray or baking dish. Let buns cool slightly and serve warm.

Coca-Cola Cake Recipe

2 cup sugar
2 cup all-purpose flour
1 cup Coca-Cola
1.5 cup small marshmallows
.5 cup butter or margarine
.5 cup vegetable oil
3 Tablespoon cocoa
1 Teaspoon baking soda
.5 cup buttermilk
2 eggs
1 teaspoon vanilla extract
.5 cup butter
3 Tablespoon cocoa
6 Tablespoon Coca-Cola
1 box (16-ounces) confectioners' sugar
1 teaspoon vanilla extract
1 cup chopped pecans

Total Time: 1hr 15min | Prep Time: 30min | Cook Time: 45min

Preheat oven to 350 degrees. In a bowl, sift the sugar and flour. Add marshmallows. In a saucepan, mix the butter, oil, cocoa and Coca-Cola. Bring to a boil and pour over dry ingredients, blend well. Dissolve baking soda in buttermilk just before adding to batter along with eggs and vanilla extract, mixing well. Pour into a well-greased 9- by-13-inch pan and bake 35 to 45 minutes. Remove from oven and frost immediately.

Coca-Cola Cake Frosting
To make frosting, combine the 1/2 cup butter, 3 tablespoons cocoa and 6 tablespoons of Coca-Cola in a saucepan. Bring to a boil and pour over confectioners' sugar, blending well. Add vanilla extract and pecans. Spread over hot cake. When cool, cut into squares and serve.

Cream Cheese Icing

1 stick butter
1 8 oz cream cheese softened
3 1/2 cups powdered sugar
Small amount of orange juice to help smooth spreading

Add nuts or coconuts to change

Crust

2 1/2 cups (297g) King Arthur Unbleached All-Purpose Flour or 2 1/2 cups (283g) Pastry Flour Blend
1 1/4 teaspoons salt*
1/4 cup (46g) vegetable shortening
10 tablespoons (142g) very cold unsalted butter
6 to 10 tablespoons (85g to 142g) ice water**
*Reduce the salt to 1 teaspoon if you use salted butter.
**Use the lesser amount of water if you use Pastry Flour Blend.
Topping (optional)
2 teaspoons milk
1 tablespoon coarse sparkling sugar

Add the butter to the flour mixture, and work it in roughly with your fingers, a pastry cutter, or a mixer. Don't be too thorough; the mixture should be quite uneven, with big chunks of butter in among the smaller ones. People get nervous about pie crust, and in their anxiety, they tend to work the dough too much. Working the butter in completely makes a mealy crust rather than a flaky one.

Drizzle 4 tablespoons of water over the flour mixture, tossing gently to combine.

Add enough additional water to make a chunky, fairly cohesive mixture. It should hold together when you gather a bit up and squeeze it in your hand. Beware of kneading the pastry too much and/or adding too much water, as this will toughen the crust.

Gently shape the pastry into a cohesive mass. Or before shaping, take it a step further: Transfer the shaggy mixture to a piece of parchment paper. Press it into a rough rectangle and fold the dough into thirds, like a business letter. If necessary, spritz any dry areas with cold water and flatten and fold again, repeating the process until all errant bits of dough have been incorporated. Folding the dough in this fashion will create more flaky layers in your final crust.

Divide the dough in half. Gather each piece into a rough disk. Smooth the disks; it's OK if they have a few cracks in the surface. Smooth their edges by running the disks along a floured surface like a wheel.

Wrap the crusts in plastic or your favorite reusable storage wrap. Chill for 30 minutes, or up to overnight. Or wrap in aluminum foil over the plastic, and freeze for up to two months.

When you're ready to make pie, remove the crusts from the refrigerator or freezer, leaving them wrapped. Allow to thaw (if frozen) or warm a bit (if chilled longer than 30 minutes), until softened enough to roll but still cold to the touch.

Place the crust on a floured work surface; our <u>silicone rolling mat</u> is a fine choice. To make a standard 9" pie, roll one piece of the pastry into a 12" to 13" round. Move the crust around on the work surface occasionally to make sure it's not sticking; add extra flour underneath as needed.

Lightly grease the pie pan with non-stick spray; this will make taking the slices out of the pan easier later. Fold the crust in quarters and place it in the pan. Or you can simply pick it up with a <u>large spatula</u> and move it that way.

For a single-crust pie, fold the edge of the crust under itself, gently squeezing it together. Crimp as desired. It's nice to make a tall crimp, as the filling for a single-crust pie is usually fairly liquid (think pumpkin or custard), and it's good to have that tall "dam".

For a double-crust pie, use a pair of scissors to trim the bottom crust to within 1/2" of the rim of the pan. Once you've added the filling, roll the top crust into a 12" circle and center it over the filling.

Bring the top crust down and over the edge of the bottom crust, pressing the two together to make a ridge of dough around the inside rim of the pan.

Using the tines of a fork, gently press the crust down onto the pan's rim all the way around the circumference of the pie. Or make a taller "finger crimp": Using the pointer finger of one hand on one side of the ridge of dough, and the thumb and pointer finger of the other hand on the other side, press to make even indentations along the entire edge of the pie crust. At this point, it helps to return the pie to the refrigerator for 20 to 30 minutes; this chills the fat, which ultimately increases the crust's flakiness.

Just before baking, brush the crust with milk or water and sprinkle it with coarse sparkling sugar, cinnamon-sugar, or granulated sugar, if desired. Make a series of cuts in the top crust to allow steam to escape. Three or four simple parallel cuts are fine, but feel free to do something more decorative if you like.

Bake according to the pie recipe's directions. Enjoy!

Tips from our Bakers

Want to make this gluten-free? For great results, substitute King Arthur Gluten-Free Measure for Measure Flour for the all-purpose flour in this recipe, no further ingredient changes necessary. Be sure to bake thoroughly; gluten-free baked goods often need a bit more time in the oven.

To keep the bottom crust from getting soggy, try brushing it with egg white and chilling before adding the filling.

You can also use melted butter to create a barrier between the fillings moisture and the crust.

Looking for a pie crust recipe that doesn't use shortening? Try our All-Butter Pie Crust.

If you're using an odd-sized pan, here's how to determine what diameter to roll your crust. Measure the pans bottom diameter, then up the sides. If your pan is 7" across the bottom, and 1 ½" up each side, that's a total of 10". This means you should roll your bottom crust to a diameter of about 12", which gives you enough extra for crimping the edges.

Be sure to use cold butter and ice water when making the crust; it helps keep the butter and shortening from dispersing throughout the dough, which in turn helps keep the crust flaky. Also, resting the dough in the refrigerator, both after mixing and rolling out, will dramatically increase the quality of your results. This "time out" both allows the gluten in the dough to relax (making the crust more tender), and firms up the fats in the dough (helping it stay flakier).

Easy Chocolate Cake

2 cups white sugar
1 3/4 cups all-purpose flour
3/4 cup unsweetened cocoa powder
1 1/2 teaspoons baking soda
1 1/2 teaspoons baking powder
1 teaspoon salt
2 eggs
1 cup milk
1/2 cup vegetable oil
2 teaspoons vanilla extract
1 cup boiling water

Preheat oven to 350 degrees F (175 degrees C). Grease and flour two 9 inch cake pans (I just made mine in 9x13 baking pan and increased bake time to 42 minutes)

In a medium bowl, stir together the sugar, flour, cocoa, baking soda, baking powder and salt. Add the eggs, milk, oil and vanilla, mix for 3 minutes with an electric mixer.

Stir in the boiling water by hand (make sure you mix it in well... the batter will look runny but have faith... it'll turn out!) Pour evenly into the greased pan(s).

Bake for 30 to 35 minutes in the preheated oven, until a toothpick inserted comes out clean. (For the 9x13 cake pan I baked it for about 42 minutes... do the toothpick test, it should come out fairly clean).

Cool for 10 minutes before removing from pans to cool completely. (I just leave mine in the pan)

Homemade Chocolate Butter Cream Frosting
3/4 cup butter
1 1/2 cups unsweetened cocoa powder
5 1/3 cups confectioners' sugar
2/3 cup milk
1 teaspoon vanilla extract

Cream butter until light and fluffy. Stir in the cocoa and confectioners' sugar alternately with the milk and vanilla (I preferred a little less cocoa). Beat to a spreading consistency.

Coconut Cream Pie

1 cup sweetened flake coconut
3 cups half-and-half
2 eggs, beaten
3/4 cup white sugar
1/2 cup all-purpose flour
1/4 teaspoon salt
1 teaspoon vanilla extract
1 (9 inch) pie shell, baked
1 cup frozen whipped topping, thawed

Preheat oven to 350 degrees F (175 degrees C).

Spread the coconut on a baking sheet and bake it, stirring occasionally, until golden brown, about 5 minutes.

In a medium saucepan, combine the half-and-half, eggs, sugar, flour and salt and mix well. Bring to a boil over low heat, stirring constantly. Remove the pan from the heat, and stir in 3/4 cup of the toasted coconut and the vanilla extract. Reserve the remaining coconut to top the pie.

Pour the filling into the pie shell and chill until firm, about 4 hours. Top with whipped topping and with the reserved coconut.

Source: tomatohero.com

German's Chocolate Cake

Cook time: 35 Min
Prep time: 20 Min
Serves: Makes a 9 x 13 or 10 x 16 sheet cake.

Pkg baker's German sweet chocolate (4 ounce)
1/2 c water
c all-purpose flour, sifted, then measured
1 tsp baking soda
1/4 tsp salt
c butter, softened
c sugar
4 large egg yolks, room temperature (reserve whites)
1 tsp vanilla extract
1 c buttermilk
4 large egg whites, beaten to form stiff peaks

Coconut Pecan Filling and Crust

1 can(s) evaporated milk 12-ounce size (not sweetened condensed)
1 1/2 c sugar
3/4 c melted butter (1 1/2 sticks)
4 large egg yolks, slightly beaten
1 1/2 tsp vanilla extract
7 oz baker's angel flake coconut
1 1/2 c broken pecans

Preheat oven to 350 degrees. Grease and flour a 9 x 13 or a 10 x 16 baking pan. If you prefer a thinner cake, use the larger pan. You may also use three 9" pans and frost between the layers.

Sift two cups flour and then measure again for accuracy. Stir in baking soda and salt and set aside. Microwave chocolate in the water until chocolate is melted, about 1 minute and 30 seconds, depending on microwave. Remove from microwave and stir well, set aside.

Separate eggs. Beat egg whites until stiff peaks form and set aside.

Using a hand mixer, beat butter and sugar just until combined. Add egg yolks one at a time, mixing after each addition.

Slowly add melted chocolate to butter mixture while mixing. Scrape sides of bowl with spatula and mix well. Add vanilla and mix well.

Add flour mixture alternately with buttermilk, beginning and ending with flour mixture. DO NOT USE A MIXER ON THIS PART! Stir by hand using a spatula or spoon. Once mixed, you may use your hand mixer for no more than 10-20 seconds, just to make sure batter is mixed well.

German Chocolate Sheet Cake (from the 1950's)
Fold in beaten egg whites. Pour into prepared pan and bake for 30 to 40 minutes or until toothpick inserted in center comes out clean.

FOR THE FROSTING: Melt butter in heavy saucepan. Add milk, sugar, vanilla and egg yolks and cook over medium heat for about 12 minutes, stirring constantly until thickened. Remove from heat and add coconut and pecans. Stir until combined. Pour warm frosting over cooled cake.

SPECIAL NOTE: If you're making the three 9" layers, you'll want to let the frosting cool a bit to thicken.

Its roots can be traced back to 1852 when American baker Samuel **German** developed a type of dark baking **chocolate** for the Baker's **Chocolate** Company. ... The possessive form (**German's**) was dropped in subsequent publications, forming the "**German Chocolate** Cake" identity and giving the false impression of a **German** origin.

Gigi's Coconut Pie

4 cups milk
1 cup sugar
1/2 cup flour
3 eggs beaten well
1/4 tsp salt
1 tsp vanilla
1/2 tsp coconut extract
1 tsp butter
2 cups shredded coconut
1 pastry shell

Heat milk in microwave for 4 minutes. In a separate bowl blend flour, sugar and salt. Gradually stir flour into heated milk. Return mixture to. Microwave for 3 to 4 minutes. Gradually stir about 1/4 mixture into eggs in a separate bowl and beat adding this back to milk. Continue to cook in microwave another 3 1/2 to 4 minutes. When thickened add butter, vanilla extract and coconut extract. Add 2 cups shredded coconut. Place clear wrap over mixture and chill. Bake pie shell.

Gigi's Crust

2 cups all-purpose flour
1/3 + tbs Crisco
1 tsp salt
6 tbs ice water

Great Grandma's Coconut Cream Pie

Beverley Williams
This recipe was my husband's great grandmother, Mrs. Cecil Walston's pie recipe.

Cook time: 1 hr 10 min
Prep time: 20 min
Serves: 6-8

Ingredients
1 c milk
1 c sweetened, flaked coconut
1 c light cream
1/2 c sugar
2 Tbsp corn starch
2 eggs, separated 1 tsp vanilla 1 pie crust.
8 oz whipped cream pre-made pie crust

Bake pie crust according to directions on package and cool completely.

Place milk and light cream in a double boiler. Add sugar and bring to a boil. Add 2 Tbsp. cold water to corn starch. Stir well.

In a bowl beat egg yolks until they are light. Add the corn starch mixture to the yolks. Mix well. Add egg mixture to the milk mixture in the double boiler. Cook for 5 minutes, stirring constantly. Remove from heat. Add vanilla and coconut. Stir. Let stand 30 minutes.

Pour into prepared crust. Cover with plastic wrap and chill 30 minutes or until set.

Remove plastic wrap. Cover with whipped cream.

Harvest Cinnamon Rolls Recipe – Perfect Cinnamon Rolls

Recipe Type: Cinnamon Roll, Brunch and Breakfast, Bread
Yields: 15 Cinnamon Rolls
Prep time: 10 min
Cook time: 20 min

1 cup milk (heated approximately 1 minute in microwave)
1/4 cup warm water (110 degrees F.)
1 teaspoon pure vanilla extract
1/2 cup butter, room temperature
2 eggs, room temperature and beaten
1/2 teaspoon salt
1/2 cup granulated sugar
5 cups bread flour
1 tablespoon vital wheat gluten (optional)*
3 teaspoons instant active dry yeast (I use SAF Instant Active Dry Yeast)
Cinnamon Filling (see recipe below) Butter Frosting (see recipe below)

* The Vital Wheat Gluten helps the sweet bread dough rise better, be more elastic, and easier to roll out. I have made these cinnamon rolls both with and without this ingredient with excellent results.

Butter a 9 x 13 x 2-inch baking pan; set aside.

After dough has risen, using your rolling pin, roll and stretch the dough into approximately a 15 x 24-inch rectangle.

Brush the 1/2 cup softened butter (listed below in the Cinnamon Filling) over the top of the dough with a rubber spatula or a pastry brush. Sprinkle Cinnamon Filling over the butter on the prepared dough. Starting with long edge, roll up dough, pinch seams to seal. NOTE: Rolling the log too tightly will result in cinnamon rolls whose centers pop up above the rest of them as they bake.

With a knife, lightly mark roll into 1 1/2-inch section. Use a sharp knife (I like to use a serrated knife and saw very gently) or slide a 12-inch piece of dental floss or heavy thread underneath. By bringing the ends of the floss up and crisscrossing them at the top of each mark, you can cut through the roll by pulling the strings in opposite directions. Place cut side up in prepared baking pan, flattening them only slightly. The unbaked cinnamon rolls should not touch each other before rising and baking. Do not pack the unbaked cinnamon rolls together.

Cinnamon Filling
1/2 cup butter, melted or softened
1 cup firmly packed brown sugar
4 to 5 tablespoons ground cinnamon
3/4 to 1 cup chopped nuts (optional)

Soften the butter; set aside. In a bowl, combine brown sugar and cinnamon; stir in chopped nuts (optional). NOTE: I like to sift the brown sugar and cinnamon together to remove any lumps.

Butter Frosting
2 ounces cream cheese, room temperature
1/4 cup butter, room temperature
1 cup powdered (confectioners) sugar
1/2 teaspoons pure vanilla extract
1/8 teaspoon lemon extract or oil (optional)

In a medium bowl, combine cream cheese and butter until creamy. Add powdered sugar, vanilla extract, and lemon extract or oil until well mixed and creamy. Refrigerate frosting until ready to use and then bring to room temperature before spreading.

Helen Huff Butterscotch Pie

1 tb cornstarch
1 lg butterscotch pie filling
1 cup white sugar
1/2 cup brown sugar
1 whole egg + 2 yokes (save whites for meringue)
1cup 2% milk
1 cup evaporated milk
1 tb butter

Mix, cook and cool. Pour into cooled pie shell

Hershey Brownies

1/2 cup butter (no substitutes, melt in microwave)
1 cup granulated sugar
4 eggs
1 teaspoon vanilla extract
1 cup flour
1 (16 ounce) cans Hershey's syrup

Icing
1 cup chopped nuts (optional)
3 cups confectioners' sugar
1/2 cup butter, melted (no subs)
4 tablespoons cocoa
4 tablespoons milk
1 teaspoon vanilla extract

Preheat oven to 350 degrees. Grease the bottom of a 10 by 15-inch pan

After melting butter in microwave, cream sugar and butter together. Add eggs, one at a time and beating well after each addition.

Add vanilla extract. Add flour, mix well. Add Hershey syrup, mix well. Add chopped nuts, if using.

Pour batter into pan. Bake for 35-40 minutes or until brownies test done with a toothpick.

When the brownies are almost done baking, prepare icing.
Bring to boil in the microwave, the butter, cocoa and 1 T. milk.

In a mixing bowl, add confectioners' sugar. Add the cocoa mixture to the sugar and beat well. Add 1 t. vanilla extract. Add the rest of the milk. Add enough to get the desired spreading consistency.

Let brownies cool about 5-10 minutes. Spread icing on brownies. Sprinkle with some more chopped nuts, if desired. The icing will harden to a fudge-like consistency.

Let brownies cool completely before cutting into squares.

Hershey's Chocolate Cake

2 cups sugar
1 3/4 cups all-purpose flour
3/4 cup Hershey's cocoa
1 1/2 tsp baking powder
1 1/2 tsp baking soda
1 tsp salt
2 eggs
1 cup milk
1/2 cup vegetable oil
2 tsp vanilla extract
1 cup boiling water

Heat oven to 350 degrees. Grease and flower baking pans.

Combine dry ingredients in a mixing bowl. Add eggs milk, oil, vanilla and beat on med speed for two minutes. Sir in boiling water (batter will be thin). Pour into pan(s).

Bake at 350 for 30-35 minutes or until wooded toothpick comes out clean. Cool ten minutes and remove to wire racks if stacking round cake. Cool completely and ice.

Hershey's "Perfectly Chocolate Icing"
1/2 cup butter melted
2/3 cup Hershey's Cocoa
3 cups powdered sugar
1/3 cup milk
1 tsp vanilla extract

Melt butter. Stir in Cocoa. Alternately add powdered sugar and milk. Beat to spreading consistency. Add small amount of additional milk if needed. Stir in vanilla. Makes two cups frosting.

Cream Cheese Icing
1/2 cup unsalted butter, softened
1 package (8 oz) cream cheese, softened
1 teaspoon vanilla
3 cups powdered sugar, plus more as needed

In large bowl, beat softened butter and cream cheese with electric mixer on medium speed 2 to 3 minutes, scraping bowl occasionally, until smooth and creamy. Stir in vanilla, then stir in powdered sugar. Add more powdered sugar as needed until frosting is a thick spreadable consistency.

Small Pan Version 8x8
1.5 cups sugar
1 1/3 cups all-purpose flour
1/2 cup +1 tbs Hershey's cocoa
1 1/8 tsp baking powder
1 1/8 tsp baking soda
3/4 tsp salt
2 eggs
3/4 cup milk
1/3 cup vegetable oil
1 1/2 tsp vanilla extract
3/4 cup boiling water

I've been looking for this recipe for a long time now...

Granny's Old-Fashioned Bread Pudding with Vanilla Sauce

4 cups (8 slices) cubed white bread
1/2 cup raisins
2 cups milk
1/4 cup butter
1/2 cup sugar
2 eggs, slightly beaten
1 tablespoon vanilla
1/2 teaspoon ground nutmeg

Sauce
1/2 cup butter
1/2 cup sugar
1/2 cup firmly packed brown sugar
1/2 cup heavy whipping cream
1 tablespoon vanilla

Pudding
Heat oven to 350°F. Combine bread and raisins in large bowl. Combine milk and 1/4 cup butter in 1-quart saucepan. Cook over medium heat until butter is melted (4 to 7 minutes). Pour milk mixture over bread; let stand 10 minutes. Stir in all remaining pudding ingredients. Pour into greased 1 1/2-quart casserole. Bake for 40 to 50 minutes or until set in center.

Sauce
Combine all sauce ingredients except vanilla in 1-quart saucepan. Cook over medium heat, stirring occasionally, until mixture thickens and comes to a full boil (5 to 8 minutes). Stir in vanilla. To serve, spoon warm pudding into individual dessert dishes; serve with sauce. Store refrigerated

Ingredients

Cake
1 stick butter, room temperature
1/2 c shortening, Crisco
2 c sugar
5 egg yolk
5 egg whites, stiffly beaten-like meringue
2 c cake flour
1 tsp soda
1 c buttermilk
1 tsp vanilla
1 c pecan nuts, chopped
1 can(s) coconut, I usually use 1 bag complete coconut flakes

Creamed Cheese Frosting
8 oz packaged cream cheese
1 tsp vanilla
1 box powered sugar (3 3/4 cups)
1/2 stick butter

Kentucky Butter Poke Cake

3 c all-purpose flour
1 tsp baking powder
1/2 tsp baking soda
1/2 tsp salt
1 c unsalted butter
2 c sugar
1 c milk
1 Tbsp white vinegar
4 large eggs
2 tsp vanilla

Butter Glaze
1 c sugar
1/2 c unsalted butter
3 Tbsp brandy (water can be substituted)
1 tsp vanilla extract

Preheat oven to 350 degrees. Generously grease and flour a 10 inch bundt pan (12 cup).

In a large bowl whisk together flour, baking powder, baking soda and salt.

Cream butter and sugar until light and fluffy; approximately 5 minutes.

Mix milk and vinegar together in separate small bowl or measuring cup.

Add eggs one at a time to butter/sugar mixture stirring just until incorporated.

Add the vanilla. Stir in milk/vinegar mixture and dry ingredients in intervals alternating between the two: stirring just until combined. Spoon into prepared bundt pan. Bake for 50-60 minutes or until a toothpick inserted in center comes out clean. Remove from the oven but do not remove from the pan.

Poke holes in the butter cake using the smaller end of a chopstick or similar sized instrument. Go close but not all the way through to the bottom. In small saucepan add sugar, butter and brandy. Place over medium low heat and stir very frequently until melted. Do not allow to boil. Remove from heat and stir in vanilla. Slowly and carefully pour over poked holes. Allow the cake to cool for 30 minutes from the time of removing it from the oven before inverting.

Lindy's Cheesecake

Crust
1 cup all-purpose flour
1 egg yolk, room temp
1/4 cup sugar
1/2 cup butter, softened
1-1/2 tsp. lemon zest (I used a micro plane grater)

Filling
24 oz. Philadelphia cream cheese, softened
16 oz. Philadelphia Neufchatel cheese, softened (recipe calls for 40 oz. of cream cheese)
1-3/4 cups sugar
1-1/2 tsp. ea. lemon zest and orange zest
5 eggs plus 2 egg yolks, room temp
1 tsp. pure vanilla extract (recipe calls for 1/2 tsp.)
1 Tbsp. lemon juice (recipe does not call for lemon juice)
1/4 cup heavy cream, room temp
3 Tbsp. flour

Place all dough ingredients in food processor and pulse several times till dough starts to leave sides of processor. If dough is too dry and doesn't come together, just add a teaspoon or more of lemon juice and pulse again. Wrap dough in plastic wrap and chill in fridge at least one hour. Preheat oven to 400 degrees. Remove ring from 9" springform pan. Roll almost a half of the dough on lightly floured wax paper to about 1/8 thickness and place on bottom of pan. (Alternately, you can just press the dough onto the pan, conforming to fit.)

Trim edges to fit and bake in preheated oven 8-12 minutes, checking at 8 minutes. Remove when dough is a light golden brown. Cool. Place the springform sides over the baked base. Roll the remaining dough about 1/8 inch thick and cut to fit sides of pan. It will be easier if you butter the sides first. This will give the dough something to cling to. Be sure you seal the base. Just lightly press the new dough to overlap slightly on the base. When you are all done, take a plastic knife and trim the dough so that it comes a generous 3/4 of the way up the sides of the pan.

Turn the oven to 550 degrees (or 525 if you are using dark or coated pan). Be sure all your ingredients are at room temperature. Don't rush this process. Place 1 block of cheese and 1/3 cup of sugar in the food processor and blend smooth for about 10 seconds. Continue with additional blocks of cheese and sugar till all are processed. Add the lemon and orange zests and the 2 egg yolks and process again till smooth. Add the remaining 5 eggs, one at a time, processing till smooth after each addition. Add heavy cream and vanilla, processing till smooth. Lastly, add flour and just pulse briefly till combined.

Pour into prepared pan and bake in preheated oven for 12 minutes, then, without opening oven door, reduce temperature to 250 (or 225 for dark or coated pans) and continue to bake for one more hour. Check the cake for doneness by jiggling pan. If it wiggles, close the oven door and leave in oven for 15-30 minutes longer. When cake no longer wiggles, it is done.

Remove to cake rack to cool. Cool completely before covering and placing in fridge overnight. May be frozen for up to 6 months.

Melt in Your Mouth Strawberry Buttermilk Pound Cake

1/2 cup shortening
1/2 cup butter
2 cups granulated sugar
3 ounce package strawberry gelatin (I used Jello brand)
5 large eggs at room temperature
1 cup buttermilk (whole milk can be used) at room temperature
3 cups all-purpose flour
1/2 teaspoon salt
2 and 1/2 teaspoon baking powder
1 tablespoon vanilla extract

Sift flour, salt, and baking powder together.

Preheat oven to 325 degrees. Prepare a 10-inch bundt pan with solid vegetable shortening then sugar or flour.

In the bowl of a stand mixer, cream together shortening and butter. Add sugar and mix until fluffy. Next mix eggs in one at a time until yellow mixes in the batter. Add vanilla and mix in the batter. Add strawberry gelatin to the flour mixture. Whisk to combine.

Add flour mixture alternately with buttermilk, beginning and ending with flour mixture. (1/3 flour mixture, 1/2 buttermilk, 1/3 flour, 1/2 buttermilk, 1/3 flour) Pour batter into a bundt pan and smooth top. Bake in 325-degree oven 65 to 70 minutes.

Allow cake to cool for 10 - 15 minutes then carefully turn out on a serving tray.

Milky Way Cake

11 Milky Way candy bars
3 sticks margarine (no, don't go and try to use butter)
2 cups sugar
4 eggs
2 1/2 cups flour
1 teaspoon baking soda
1 cup buttermilk
2 1/2 teaspoons vanilla
1/2 cup chopped nuts (I used pecans)
2 cups powdered sugar

Melt 8 Milky Way candy bars and 1 stick of margarine until smooth; set aside.

Cream sugar and 1 stick margarine. Add eggs, one at a time, beating until smooth. Add flour, buttermilk and soda. Add Milky Way bar mix and 2 teaspoons vanilla and chopped nuts.

Bake in a greased and floured bundt pan, or angel food pan for 50-60 minutes at 325 degrees.

Icing
Melt the remaining 3 Milky Way candy bars and remaining stick of margarine until smooth. Add 1/2 teaspoon vanilla, 2 cups powdered sugar. (If too dry, add a small amount of milk) Spread on cooled cake.

Say your prayers before eating and ask the Lord for restraint!

Momma's Boiled Custard

1 gallon milk
5 tbs Vanilla (or to taste)
12 eggs yolks
3 cups sugar
3 tbs flour
Pinch salt

Separate egg yolks and set whites aside. Beat eggs until blended. Separate 1/4 cup milk and mix with flour beat with a whisk until smooth. Warm milk in double boiler and add flour and egg mixture along with sugar and salt, cook over medium heat until thickened, stirring often do not boil. Remove from heat, beat vigorously with whisk add vanilla and Chill.

2012
I made this Christmas 2012 and it was too thick. Blended it with some milk and it was fine. I also forgot to separate eggs, and the whites caused some curdling action the blender smoothed it out. I used a large cooker and cooked it 200 degrees. Brenda said that momma would whip the egg whites and fold it back in at the end.

Boiled Custard & Ice Cream
(for homemade ice cream pour chilled custard into ice cream freezer)
½ gallon milk
6 eggs
1 1/2 cup sugar
3 tablespoons flour
1 tablespoon vanilla

Over medium heat warm milk. Using electric mixer combine eggs, sugar and flour. Pour this mixture into milk overheat. Cook, stirring constantly until spoon is coated when lifted out of custard. Set pan in cool water and stir to cool custard more quickly. Strain. Stir in vanilla, continue cooling in refridge.

Most Amazing Chocolate Cake
Rachel Farnsworth

Prep time 10 mins
Cook Time 35 mins
Time to Make It 45 mins
Yield 3 9-inch rounds

Notes
The better quality cocoa powder you use, the better the cake.

Butter and flour for coating and dusting the cake pan
3 cups all-purpose flour
3 cups granulated sugar
1 1/2 cups unsweetened cocoa powder
1 tablespoon baking soda
1 1/2 teaspoons baking powder
1 1/2 teaspoons salt
4 large eggs
1 1/2 cups buttermilk
1 1/2 cups warm water
1/2 cup vegetable oil
2 teaspoons vanilla extract

Preheat oven to 350 degrees.

Butter three 9-inch cake rounds. Dust with flour and tap out the excess.

Mix together flour, sugar, cocoa, baking soda, baking powder, and salt in a stand mixer using a low speed until combined.

Add eggs, buttermilk, warm water, oil, and vanilla. Beat on a medium speed until smooth. This should take just a couple of minutes.

Divide batter among the three pans. I found that it took just over 3 cups of the batter to divide it evenly.

Bake for 30-35 minutes until the cake meets the toothpick test (stick a toothpick in and it comes out clean).

Cool on wire racks for 15 minutes and then turn out the cakes onto the racks and allow to cool completely.

Frost with your favorite frosting and enjoy!

Chocolate Cream Cheese Buttercream

Prep time 10 mins
Time to Make It 10 mins

This recipe makes enough frosting to frost a 3-layer cake.

1 1/2 cups butter, softened
8 oz cream cheese, softened
1 1/2 cups unsweetened cocoa powder
3 teaspoons vanilla extract
7-8 cups powdered sugar
About 1/4 cup milk (as needed)

In a large bowl, beat together butter and cream cheese until fluffy. Use a hand mixer or stand mixer for best results.

Add in cocoa powder and vanilla extract. Beat until combined.

Beat in powdered sugar, 1 cup at a time. Add milk as necessary to make a spreadable consistency. The frosting should be very thick and will thicken even more if refrigerated.

Notes
Extra dark cocoa will result in a much darker, almost black frosting.

Old Fashion Pie

6.5 oz pudding and pie filling
12 oz can carnation evaporated milk 3/4 cup milk

Create pie crust using "ten-minute" pie crust recipe. Bake at 425 for 10 to fifteen minutes until golden brown. Set aside and cool.

In a nonstick pan on med heat mix large cook and serve favorite pie filling, 1 can evaporated milk 3/4 regular milk. Stir constantly until mixture comes to a full boil and cool for 10 minutes stirring three times.

When cool pour into pie shell and chill well.

Mix 1 cup whipping cream, 2 Tb. sugar, or powdered sugar and 1/2 tsp. pure vanilla extract. Whip cream till it holds a firm shape. Top pie with cream.

Old Fashion Bread Pudding

4 cups (8 slices) cubed white bread
1/2 cup raisins
2 cups milk
1/4 cup butter
1/2 cup sugar
2 eggs, slightly beaten
1 tablespoon vanilla
1/2 teaspoon ground nutmeg

Sauce
1/2 cup butter
1/2 cup sugar
1/2 cup firmly packed brown sugar
1/2 cup heavy whipping cream
1 tablespoon vanilla

Heat oven to 350°F. Combine bread and raisins in large bowl. Combine milk and 1/4 cup butter in 1-quart saucepan. Cook over medium heat until butter is melted (4 to 7 minutes).

Pour milk mixture over bread; let stand 10 minutes.

Stir in all remaining pudding ingredients. Pour into greased 1 1/2-quart casserole. Bake for 40 to 50 minutes or until set in center.

Old Fashion Bread Pudding - 2

I baked for 1 hour at 350 in bread pan turned out

Pudding
4 cups white bread, cubed, about 8 slices
1/2 cup raisins
2 cups milk
1/4 cup butter
1/2 cup sugar
2 eggs, slightly beaten
1 tablespoon vanilla
1/2 teaspoon ground nutmeg

Sauce
1/2 cup butter
1/2 cup sugar
1/2 cup firmly packed brown sugar
1/2 cup heavy whipping cream
1 tablespoon vanilla

Pudding
Heat oven to 350°F.

Combine bread and raisins in large bowl.

Combine milk and 1/4 cup butter in 1-quart saucepan. Cook over medium heat until butter is melted, about 4 to 7 minutes. Pour milk mixture over bread; let stand 10 minutes.

Stir in all remaining pudding ingredients. Pour into greased 1 1/2-quart casserole. Bake for 40 to 50 minutes or until set in center.

Sauce
Combine all sauce ingredients except vanilla in 1-quart saucepan. Cook over

medium heat, stirring occasionally until mixture thickens and comes to a full boil, about 5 to 8 minutes. Stir in vanilla.

To serve, spoon warm pudding into individual dessert dishes; serve with sauce. Store any leftovers in the refrigerator.

Old Fashion Custard Pie

1 unbaked pie shell (I use Marie Callendar's deep dish)
3 large eggs
½ cup of sugar
½ teaspoon of salt
½ teaspoon of nutmeg
2-2/3 cups of milk
1 teaspoon pure vanilla extract

Pre-heat the oven to 350 degrees. Beat your eggs slightly, then add sugar, salt, nutmeg, and milk. Beat well and poor into the unbaked pie shell. Bake for 35 to 40 minutes. Remove from oven and cool. Sprinkle the top of pie with fresh ground nutmeg and serve.

Orange Dream-sicle Cake

Cake
5 eggs
3 cups self rising flour
3/4 lb butter, softened (3/4 LB of butter equals 3 sticks)
3 cups sugar
3/4 cup carbonated orange soda beverage, any brand
1/2 teaspoon Salt
2 drops Orange Food Coloring (optional)
1 Tablespoon Orange Zest

Glaze
3 cups confectioners' sugar
1/4 cup Orange soda
1 tablespoon Orange Juice
1 teaspoon Orange Zest

NOTE: You need to use a LARGE bundt pan or a tube pan for this recipe. Do NOT fill more than two-thirds full because it does rise more than a regular cake due to the soda added. You will have extra batter, so I usually use it to bake cupcakes.

Mix butter and sugar together for about 10 minutes. Add in your eggs-1 at a time, beating after each is added in. Add in flour, salt, zest & food coloring. Fold in your orange soda of choice. Pour into well-greased 12-cup Bundt pan or large 12 cup or more tube pan. Bake at 325 degrees for 1 to 1 hour & 15 min or until fully set. Remove from oven and transfer to wire rack to cool, then drizzle your glaze on top

To get the DEEP orange color that dips into the center, you see on my cake, I used a separate bowl (once all batter was ready to be poured into the pan) removed about one cup of the batter, placed it in the bowl and added an extra drop of orange food coloring and a little pinch more orange zest, I then poured this FIRST, into my pan, before adding the rest of the batter.

Glaze (This is optional)
Combine all the glaze ingredients in a small bowl and whisk until the glaze is pretty thick, adding more or less liquid/powdered sugar so you can get the correct consistency. Drizzle glaze all over the cake.

ENJOY!

Pate Brisee Recipe

2 1/2 cups (350 grams) all-purpose flour
1 teaspoon (4 grams) salt
1 tablespoon (14 grams) granulated white sugar
1 cup (2 sticks) (226 grams) unsalted butter, chilled, and cut into 1 inch (2.5 cm) pieces
1/4 to 1/2 cup (60 - 120 ml) ice water

In a food processor, place the flour, salt, and sugar, and process until combined. Add the butter and process until the mixture resembles coarse meal (about 15 seconds). Pour 1/4 cup (60 ml) water in a slow, steady stream, through the feed tube until the dough just holds together when pinched. Add remaining water, if necessary. Do not process more than 30 seconds.

Turn the dough out onto your work surface and gather it into a ball. Divide the dough into two equal pieces, flatten each portion into a disk, cover with plastic wrap, and refrigerate for 30 minutes to one hour before using. This will chill the butter and allow the gluten in the flour to relax. At this point you can also freeze the dough for later use.

For each disk of pastry, on a lightly floured surface, roll out the pastry to fit into a 8 or 9 inch (20 to 23 cm) tart or pie pan. To prevent the pastry from sticking to the counter and to ensure uniform thickness, keep lifting up and turning the pastry a quarter turn as you roll (always roll from the center of the pastry outwards to get uniform thickness). To make sure it is the right size, take your tart or pie pan, flip it over, and place it on the rolled out pastry. The pastry should be about an inch larger than your pan.

When the pastry is rolled to the desired size, lightly roll pastry around your rolling pin, dusting off any excess flour as you roll. Unroll onto the top of your tart or pie pan. Never pull the pastry or you will get shrinkage (shrinkage is caused by too much pulling of the pastry when placing it in the pan). Gently lay in pan and with a small floured piece of pastry, lightly press pastry into bottom and up sides of pan. If using a tart pan, roll your rolling pin over top of pan to get rid of excess pastry. If using a pie pan, flute the edges of the pastry. The pastry is now ready to use.

To prebake the tart or pie shell: With the tines of a fork, prick the bottom of the dough (this will prevent the dough from puffing up as it bakes). Cover and refrigerate for 20 minutes to chill the butter and to rest the gluten.

Preheat oven to 400 degrees F (205 degrees C) and place rack in center of oven. Line the unbaked pastry shell with parchment paper or aluminum foil. Fill tart or pie pan with pie weights, rice, or beans, making sure the weights are to the top of the pan and evenly distributed over the entire surface. Bake crust for about 20 to 25 minutes or until the crust is dry and lightly browned. Remove weights and cool crust on wire rack. Proceed with desired recipe that calls for a pre-baked shell.

Read more:
http://www.joyofbaking.com/PateBrisee.html#ixzz2japXQWWX

Payday Bars

3 cups salted peanuts (no skins), divided
2 & 1/2 tablespoons butter
2 cups peanut butter chips
14 ounces sweetened condensed milk 2 cups miniature marshmallows kosher salt or sea salt, optional

Place 1 & 1/2 cups peanuts in the bottom of an ungreased 11"x 7" pan. Melt butter and peanut butter chips in a large saucepan over low heat. Stir until smooth.

Remove from heat. Stir in condensed milk and marshmallows. Continue stirring until smooth and well-blended.

Pour peanut butter mixture over peanuts in pan. Sprinkle remaining 1 & 1/2 cups peanuts over top of peanut butter mixture.

If saltier bars are desired, sprinkle lightly with salt.

Cover and refrigerate until chilled. Then, cut into bars. Bars can be served chilled or at room temperature.

Notes:
These can be made in a 9"x 13" pan. Use another cup of peanuts, divided between the bottom of the pan and the top of the bars. The same amount of filling will work and give you slightly thinner bars.

Peach Cobbler

2 15 oz cans of sliced peaches
1/2 can water
2 cups sugar
1 stick butter
2 cups Bisquick
1 cup milk
1 tbs vanilla

On the stove bring peaches, water and 1 cup sugar to a boil and cook for 5 minutes set aside to cool.

In a large mixing bowl, combine Bisquick, sugar, milk, 3/4 stick butter and vanilla stir until blended.

Place remaining 1/4 stick melted butter in a pan and coat bottom. Pour batter into pan and level. Pour cooled peaches onto batter and place in a pre-heated 425-degree oven. Bake for 40 minutes and check for doneness. Bake until golden brown. Let cool and set

Pound Cake

Ingredients
1 cup butter room temperature
2 cups granulated sugar
4 large eggs
1 tablespoon vanilla extract
2 3/4 cups all-purpose flour
1/2 teaspoon baking powder
1/2 teaspoon baking soda
1 cup milk

Directions
Separate the eggs. Beat the whites to stiff peaks and reserve the yolks. In a large bowl, cream sugar and butter or margarine. Beat in egg yolks. Stir in milk and vanilla. Add flour, 1 cup at a time. Fold in stiffly beaten egg whites.

Bake for 90 minutes at 325 degrees F (165 degrees)

Pistachio Delight

1 oz package sugar free pudding mix
10 oz crushed pineapple
1/2 cup chopped pecans
1 tub (8oz) Whipped topping 1 cup cottage cheese
Mix together and chill

Raspberry Cream Cheese Sweet Rolls

Prep Time 20 Mins
Cook Time 30 Mins
Rising Time 2 Hrs

Light and fluffy Raspberry Cream Cheese Rolls will be your new breakfast go-to recipe. Buttery soft dough filled to the brim with a delicious raspberry cream cheese mixture and smothered in a cream cheese glaze for an over-the-top finish.

Dough
2/3 cup whole milk
5 tablespoons sugar, divided
2 teaspoons active dry yeast
2 large eggs, room temperature
2 3/4 cups all-purpose flour
1 teaspoon kosher salt
1/2 cup unsalted butter, cut into 1-inch pieces, room temperature
1/2 tablespoon unsalted butter, melted

Cream Cheese Filling
4 ounces cream cheese, softened
2 tablespoons butter, softened
1/4 cup granulated sugar
1 teaspoon vanilla

Raspberry Filling
1 1/2 cups frozen raspberries
1/2 tablespoon cornstarch

Cream Cheese Glaze
1/4 cup butter, softened
1 ounce cream cheese
1/2 teaspoon vanilla
3/4 cup powdered sugar
3 tablespoons of milk

Instructions

Dough

In a medium bowl, combine milk and 1 tablespoon sugar. Sprinkle yeast over milk and whisk to blend. Let sit until yeast is foamy, about 5 minutes. Add eggs; whisk until smooth.

Combine remaining 4 tablespoons sugar, flour, and salt in the bowl of a stand mixer fitted with a dough hook. Add the milk mixture. With the mixer running, add butter, 1 piece at a time, blending well between additions.

Knead on medium speed for 1 minute. Knead on medium-high speed until the dough is soft, about 5 minutes.

Brush a medium bowl with some melted butter; place the dough in the bowl. Brush the top of the dough with the remaining melted butter; cover with plastic wrap.

Let dough rise in a warm, draft-free area until doubled in size, about 1 hour. When you are ready, punch the dough, turn out onto a floured surface, and roll into a 10x15 rectangle (it should be about 1/4 inch thick).

Cream Cheese Filling

To make the cream cheese filling, beat together the cream cheese, butter, and sugar until smooth. Stir in the vanilla.

Raspberry Filling
Toss the raspberries in the cornstarch, evenly coating the raspberries.

Spread the cream cheese mixture over the dough. Sprinkle with the raspberries and roll up tightly starting on the long edge.

Using a very sharp knife, cut the log into 12 rolls. Place them into a greased 9x13 baking pan. Let rise in a warm place until double.

Baking
Bake at 350°F for 25-30 minutes. Remove the rolls from the oven and let them cool for 5 minutes.

Cream Cheese Glaze
While the rolls cool, in a medium bowl mix together the glaze ingredients. Add more milk if necessary to thin the glaze. Pour the glaze over the warm rolls and serve.

Raspberry Zinger Poke Cake

Prep Time 15 mins
Inactive Time 4 hrs 30 mins
Cook Time 30 mins
Yields 18-24 servings

There seems to be so many Christmas parties this time of the year, and this cake would be a fun addition! Although it's not a traditional Christmas flavor, the red and white cake with the coconut topping make it perfect for the season! Although this is the first time I have actually made this cake, I'm sure it will be a family holiday favorite for years to come!

1 box (18.25oz.) white cake mix
Ingredients listed on box to prepare cake
1 box (3 oz.) raspberry flavored gelatin (Jello)
2 cups hot water
1 jar (10 oz.) raspberry preserves
1 tub (8 oz.) Cool Whip, thawed
1 bag (7 oz.) shredded coconut

Bake the cake according to package directions using a 9x13-in. baking pan. After the cake has baked, remove from the oven and allow to cool for 30 minutes. Using the handle end of a wooden spoon or a meat fork, poke cake every inch or so with the handle of wooden spoon or tines of meat fork halfway into the cake. There is no set number of holes, but you want plenty of places to fill. Mix the raspberry gelatin with 2 cups of hot water until dissolved. Pour the Jello evenly over the cake, trying to fill the holes as much as you can. In a small bowl, microwave the raspberry preserves until easy to spread, about 30 seconds. Pour the preserves over the top of the cake and spread evenly. Top with Cool Whip. Sprinkle the shredded coconut over the top. Refrigerate for at least 4 hours before serving. Store leftovers in the refrigerator.

Sandy Apple Crisp

Serves 8
1 hour 10 minutes

Filling
6 tart apples, roughly chopped
1/2 cup brown sugar
2 tablespoons all-purpose flour
1 teaspoon cinnamon
1 teaspoon lemon juice
1/2 teaspoon nutmeg

Topping
1 cup all-purpose flour
2/3 cup old-fashioned oats
2/3 cup brown sugar, packed
1 teaspoon cinnamon
1/2 teaspoon salt
1/2 cup (1 stick) unsalted cold butter, cubed
Ice cream or whipped cream, garnish

Preheat oven to 350° F and lightly grease a springform pan with butter, then wrap the outside and bottom of pan tightly with aluminum foil.

In a medium bowl, whisk together flour, cinnamon and nutmeg, then add apples.

Pour lemon juice over apples and toss everything together until apples are thoroughly coated and dry mixture is distributed evenly on them.

Transfer apples to greased pan and set aside.

In a separate, large bowl, whisk together flour, oats, sugar, cinnamon and salt.

Add cubed butter and use two forks or a pastry cutter to cut butter in. Mixture should resemble coarse sand.

Sprinkle topping over apples and place in oven.

Bake for 45-55 minutes, or until topping is golden brown and apples are molten and bubbly.

Remove from oven and let cool 15 minutes before serving, top with ice cream or whipped cream.

Shirley Temple Cake
Larry Version

Prep Time 10 mins
Cook Time 1 Hr 30 mins
Total Time 1 Hr 40 mins

A light and delicious bundt, this Shirley Temple Cake will evoke the inner child in us. Full of lemon lime and cherry flavor this cake is truly addicting!

Course: Dessert
Cuisine: American
Servings: 12
Calories: 623 kcal

1 1/2 cups butter softened
3 cups granulated sugar
5 eggs
3 cups all-purpose flour
2 Tablespoons vanilla extract
3/4 cream soda
1 jar maraschino cherries 10 oz, drained and juice reserved **Glaze:**
2 cups powdered sugar
1 Tablespoon vanilla extract
3-4 Tablespoons milk

Preheat oven to 325.

In large bowl mix together your butter and sugar until light and fluffy. Add in your eggs and continue to mix until blended. Add in your flour and mix again until smooth. Pour in your vanilla extract and cream soda. Beat to combine. Fold in your cherries. Spread into a greased bundt pan and bake for 1 1/2 hours or until center is set.

Turn onto serving dish and let cool slightly and then using a skewer, poke holes all over the top of the cake and pour your reserved cherry juice slowly over the top making sure the juice gets soaked up.

It's ok for it to seep to the bottom to soak as well. Let cool completely. Meanwhile mix together your glaze ingredients and drizzle over the top of your cake. Top with more cherries if desired.

Snickerdoodles
Rachel Wilson Recipe

1 1/2 cups sugar
1 stick butter
1/2 cup shortening (butter flavored)
2 large eggs
2 3/4 cups all-purpose flour
2 tsp cream of tarter
1 tsp baking soda
1 tsp salt

Coating
1/4 cup sugar
2 tsp ground cinnamon

Heat oven to 400 degrees

Beat 1 1/2 cups sugar, softened butter, shortening, and eggs (with mixer on medium) stir in flour, cream of tartar, baking soda and salt. Shape dough into balls. Mix 1/4 cup sugar and 2 tsp cinnamon. Roll balls in mixture and place on cookie sheet. Bake 8 to 10 minutes. Immediately remove to wire rack to cool.

Surprise Carrot Cake

3 cups shredded carrots
1-3/4 cups sugar
1 cup canola oil
3 large eggs, room temperature
2 cups all-purpose flour
2 teaspoons baking soda
2 teaspoons ground cinnamon
1 teaspoon salt
1/2 cup chopped pecans

Filling
1 package (8 ounces) cream cheese, softened
1/4 cup sugar
1 large egg, room temperature

Frosting
1 package (8 ounces) cream cheese, softened
1/4 cup butter, softened
2 teaspoons vanilla extract
4 cups confectioners' sugar

In a large bowl, beat the carrots, sugar, oil and eggs until well blended. In a large bowl, combine the flour, baking soda, cinnamon and salt; gradually beat into carrot mixture until blended. Stir in the pecans. Pour 3 cups batter into a greased and floured 10-in. fluted tube pan.

In a small bowl, beat cream cheese and sugar until smooth. Beat in egg. Spoon over batter. Top with remaining batter.

Bake at 350° for 55-60 minutes or until a toothpick inserted in the center comes out clean. Cool for 10 minutes before removing from pan to a wire rack to cool completely.

For frosting, in a small bowl, beat the cream cheese, butter and vanilla until fluffy. Gradually add confectioners' sugar until smooth. Frost cake. Store in the refrigerator.

Ten Minute Pie Crust

Pour 1/2 cup Crisco vegetable oil in a pie pan add 1/4 cup milk, 1/2 teaspoon salt, 1 tbs sugar, 1 1/2 cup ap flour. Fold into a ball and spread into pan with fingers. Double for thicker crust.

For ten-inch fluted pie dish use:
3/4 Crisco vegetable oil
1/3 cup milk
1/3 teaspoon salt
2 tbs sugar
2 cups all-purpose flour

Toasted Coconut Tres Leches Pound Cake

1 ½ cups unsalted butter, softened
2 ½ cups sugar
1 tablespoon cornstarch
3 cups all-purpose flour, divided
8 large eggs, divided
1 cup unsweetened flaked coconut, toasted
1 teaspoon coconut extract
1 (14-ounce) can sweetened condensed milk
1 (6-ounce) can evaporated milk
1 cup coconut milk

Preheat oven to 325°. Spray a 15-cup Bundt pan with baking spray with flour.

In a large bowl, beat butter, sugar, and cornstarch with a mixer at medium speed until fluffy, 3 to 4 minutes, stopping to scrape sides of bowl. Add 1½ cups flour and 4 eggs, beating until combined. Add remaining 1½ cups flour and remaining 4 eggs, beating until combined. Beat in toasted coconut and coconut extract. Spoon batter into prepared pan. Rinse bowl.

Bake for 1 hour. Increase oven temperature to 350°, and bake for 15 minutes more.

In same bowl, combine condensed milk, evaporated milk, and coconut milk. Using a long wooden skewer, poke holes in warm cake. Slowly pour milk mixture over cake. Let cool at room temperature for 1 hour. Refrigerate until chilled before serving. Cover and refrigerate for up to 1 week.

Twinkies Recipe

2 1/2 tablespoons flour (for the cream filling)
1/2 cup milk (for the cream filling)
1/2 cup confectioners' sugar (for the cream filling)
1/2 cup cold butter (for the cream filling)
1 teaspoon banana or vanilla flavoring/extract (for the cream filling) 1/2 teaspoon salt (for the cream filling)
2 cups flour
1 tablespoon baking powder
2 teaspoons vanilla
1 cup milk, at room temperature
8 tablespoons butter, at room temperature
1 cup sugar
2 eggs, at room temperature

To make the cream filling, mix the flour and milk in a small pan and boil until thick. Cool the mixture, then beat until fluffy. Add the other four ingredients (confectioners' sugar, butter, banana/vanilla extract and salt) one at a time, beating well after each addition. Transfer to the refrigerator for 1 hour. (The cream should be cold and rather stiff when you later pipe it into the cakes, but the act of piping will soften it to the correct consistency.)

Begin making the sponge cake. Preheat the oven to 350 F and thoroughly grease 8 to 12 wells in a "Cream Canoe" pan (Rappaport recommends the Norpro 3964).

Whisk together the flour and baking powder in a bowl. Set aside. Stir the vanilla extract into the milk in a separate bowl and set that aside as well.

Cream the butter and sugar in a large bowl until fluffy. Beat the eggs into the batter one at a time, until it is very light and fluffy. Add the flour mixture alternately with the milk, beginning and ending with the flour mixture, thoroughly incorporating each addition before adding the next. Pour batter into prepared pans (Rappaport recommends filling them about halfway, as there is plenty of leavening in the batter.)

Bake for 15 minutes, or until the cakes are just becoming golden and a toothpick inserted into the center of the center cake comes out clean. Remove from the oven, invert to a wire rack and cool completely before filling.

Using a pastry bag or cream-filling gun, fill three holes on the underside of each cake with the cream. Slightly overfill the holes, then use your thumb to tamp in the cream.

Vanilla Roll Cake

2 eggs
3 egg yolks
1/2 cup (100 grams) sugar
1 teaspoon vanilla extract
1/3 cup (30 grams) sifted cake flour
3 tablespoons (30 grams) cornstarch
1/4 cup red & green Wilton batter bits or edible confetti
2 egg whites
1 tablespoon sugar

Vanilla Buttercream
1 cup butter, room temperature
3 cups (360 grams) powdered sugar
3-4 tbsp red & green sprinkles
1 teaspoon vanilla extract
1-3 teaspoons heavy cream
Decorations
4 oz white chocolate
red & green sprinkles

Vickie Crowley Butterscotch Pie

2/3 C brown sugar
2 Tbsp corn starch
1/8 tsp salt
2 C milk
2 egg yolks, beaten (keep the egg whites for the meringue)
2 Tbsp butter (I have also used margarine)
1 tsp vanilla
1 9" baked pie shell

In a large saucepan, combine the brown sugar, cornstarch and salt; gradually add the milk.

Cook mixture over medium heat, stirring constantly until mixture thickens and comes to a boil.

Boil for 1 minute, remove from heat and add 1/2 of the mixture into the beaten egg yolks stirring constantly.

Return the egg yolk mixture to the saucepan and bring to a boil again.

Remove from heat, stir in butter and vanilla then pour this into the baked pie shell. Cool pie.

Meringue (I don't really measure here! :))

Preheat oven to 350F

2 egg whites
1/4 - 1/2 C white sugar

Using an electric mixer, beat the egg whites on high until small peaks are formed.

Slowly add the sugar and continue beating until all the sugar is added and the desired peaks are formed (it usually takes me about 4 minutes or so).

Using a spatula or spoon, drop dollops of the meringue on the pie making sure to cover the entire surface of the pie to the edge.

Slide into the preheated oven and let the meringue cook until it browns.

Whipped Cream Cheese

8 ounces cream cheese, room temperature
1 cup granulated sugar
1/8 tsp. table salt
1 tsp. vanilla extract
1 1/2 cups cold heavy whipping cream

In the bowl of a stand mixer, beat whipping cream on medium high until stiff peaks form; about 3 minutes.

Place whipped cream into a separate bowl and clean out stand mixer bowl.

In clean stand mixer bowl whip cream cheese with whisk attachment until light and smooth. Add in sugar, salt and vanilla and beat until fully incorporated.

Remove bowl from stand mixer and gently fold in the whipped cream (by hand) to cream cheese mixture.

Can be used immediately. You can store in refrigerator until ready to use, just be sure to bring to room temperature before piping or spreading

Yellow Cake

2 1/4 cups all-purpose flour.
2 1/2 teaspoons baking powder.
3/4 teaspoon salt.
3/4 cup butter, softened to room temperature.
1 1/2 cups granulated sugar.
3 large eggs, room temperature.
2 teaspoons vanilla extract.
1 cup whole milk.

Preheat oven to 350 degrees F (175 degrees C). Grease and flour one 9x13 inch pan.

In a large bowl, cream sugar and shortening until light and fluffy.

Bake at 350 degrees F (175 degrees C) for 40 to 45 minutes, or until a toothpick inserted into the **cake** comes out clean.

Zucchini Banana Cake

2 cups all-purpose flour
1/2 tsp. baking soda
1 tsp. baking powder
2 tsp. ground cinnamon
½ teaspoon salt
1 cup granulated sugar
2 eggs, room temperature
1 cup vegetable oil
2 tsp. vanilla extract
2 ripe bananas
2 cups shredded zucchini, lightly drained

Cake
Heat oven to 350°F and prepare three 8-inch round cake pans.

In a large bowl sift together the flour, baking soda, baking powder, cinnamon, and salt.

In a stand mixer on low speed add in the sugar, eggs, oil, vanilla, and banana.

Mix on medium speed for about 1 minute, or until fully combined.

One cup at a time add the flour mixture into the sugar mixture. Mix until just incorporated and remove bowl from mixer.

Stir in the drained and shredded zucchini.

*I prefer to not peel the green skin off on my zucchini, but you certainly can. If you have a very large zucchini, remove any seeds prior to grating.
Bake for 22-26 minutes, or until inserted toothpick is removed mostly clean.

Dishes and Doughs

Baked Burrito Casserole

1 lb ground beef
1/2 onion, chopped
1 package taco seasoning
6 large flour tortillas
1 can refried beans
2 -3 cups shredded taco cheese or cheddar cheese
1 can cream of mushroom soup
4 ounces sour cream

Brown beef and onion; drain. Add taco seasoning and stir in refried beans.

Mix soup and sour cream in a separate bowl. Spread 1/2 sour cream mixture in the bottom of a casserole dish. Tear up 3 tortillas and spread over sour cream mixture. Put 1/2 the meat bean mixture over that. Add a layer of cheese.

Repeat the layers. Sprinkle cheese over the top and bake, uncovered, at 350°F for 20-30 minutes.

Chicken Broccoli Stir Fry

Chicken and Broccoli
1 lb chicken breast (boneless skinless), cut into ¾" pieces
2 Tbsp cooking oil (I used extra light olive oil), divided
1 lb broccoli cut into florets (about 5 cups)
1 small yellow onion sliced into strips
1/2 lb white button mushrooms thickly sliced

Stir Fry Sauce
2/3 cup **low sodium chicken broth**
3 Tbsp low sodium soy sauce or added to taste
2 Tbsp **light brown sugar** packed (or honey to taste)
1 Tbsp corn starch
1 Tbsp sesame oil
1 tsp fresh ginger peeled and grated (lightly packed)
1 tsp garlic (2 small cloves) grated
1/4 tsp **black pepper** plus more to season chicken

In a small bowl, combine all of the sauce ingredients and whisk to dissolve sugar and corn starch (warm broth will help dissolve the sugar faster). Set sauce aside.

Cut chicken into small bite-sized pieces (no more than 3/4" thick) and season lightly with pepper. Heat a large heavy skillet or wok over medium-high heat. Add 1 Tbsp oil. Add chicken in a single layer and let it sit undisturbed for 1 minute to get a good sear then stir fry for another 5 minutes or until golden brown just cooked through then remove to a bowl and loosely cover to keep warm.

In the same skillet, add another 1 Tbsp oil along with broccoli florets, sliced onion and sliced mushrooms. Stir fry 3 minutes or until mushrooms are softened and broccoli is crisp-tender then **reduce heat to medium/low.**

Give the sauce a quick stir in case there was any settling of starch and pour all of it over the vegetables. Simmer 3-4 minutes or until sauce is thickened and garlic and ginger are mellowed in flavor. To thin the sauce, add water a tablespoon at a time.

Return chicken to the pan and stir another 30 seconds or until heated through. Add more soy sauce to taste if needed and serve over hot rice.

Deep Dish Pizza

Crust
2 cups (240g) King Arthur Unbleached All-Purpose Flour
3/4 teaspoon salt
1/2 teaspoon instant yeast or active dry yeast
3/4 cup (170g) lukewarm water
1 tablespoon (13g) olive oil + 1 1/2 tablespoons (18g) olive oil for the
Topping
6 ounces (170g) mozzarella, grated (about 1 1/4 cups, loosely packed) *
1/3 to 1/2 cup (74g to 113g) tomato sauce or pizza sauce, homemade or store-bought freshly grated hard cheese and fresh herbs for sprinkling on top after baking, optional*
Pan

Weigh your flour; or measure it by gently spooning it into a cup, then sweeping off any excess.

Place the flour, salt, yeast, water, and 1 tablespoon (13g) of the olive oil in the bowl of a stand mixer or other medium-large mixing bowl.

Stir everything together to make a shaggy, sticky mass of dough with no dry patches of flour. This should take 30 to 45 seconds in a mixer using the beater paddle; or about 1 minute by hand, using a spoon or spatula. Scrape down the sides of the bowl to gather the dough into a rough ball; cover the bowl.

After 5 minutes, uncover the bowl and reach a bowl scraper or your wet hand down between the side of the bowl and the dough, as though you were going to lift the dough out. Instead of lifting, stretch the bottom of the dough up and over its top. Repeat three more times, turning the bowl 90° each time. This process of four stretches, which takes the place of kneading, is called a fold.

Re-cover the bowl, and after 5 minutes do another fold. Wait 5 minutes and repeat; then another 5 minutes and do a fourth and final fold. Cover the bowl and let the dough rest, undisturbed, for 40 minutes. Then refrigerate it for a minimum of 12 hours, or up to 72 hours. It'll rise slowly as it chills, developing flavor; this long rise will also add flexibility to your schedule.

About 3 hours before you want to serve your pizza, prepare your pan. Pour 1 1/2 tablespoons (18g) olive oil into a well-seasoned cast iron skillet that's 10" to 11" diameter across the top, and about 9" across the bottom. Heavy, dark cast iron will give you a superb crust; but if you don't have it, use another oven-safe heavy-bottomed skillet of similar size, or a 10" round cake pan or 9" square pan. Tilt the pan to spread the oil across the bottom and use your fingers or a paper towel to spread some oil up the edges, as well.

Transfer the dough to the pan and turn it once to coat both sides with the oil. After coating the dough in oil, press the dough to the edges of the pan, dimpling it using the tips of your fingers in the process. The dough may start to resist and shrink back; that's OK, just cover it and let it rest for about 15 minutes, then repeat the dimpling/pressing. At this point the dough should reach the edges of the pan; if it doesn't, give it one more 15-minute rest before dimpling/ pressing a third and final time.

Cover the crust and let it rise for 2 hours at room temperature. The fully risen dough will look soft and pillowy and will jiggle when you gently shake the pan.

About 30 minutes before baking, place one rack at the bottom of the oven and one toward the top (about 4" to 5" from the top heating element). Preheat the oven to 450°F.

When you're ready to bake the pizza, sprinkle about three-quarters of the mozzarella (a scant 1 cup) evenly over the crust. Cover the entire crust, no bare dough showing; this will yield caramelized edges.

Dollop small spoonfuls of the sauce over the cheese; laying the cheese down first like this will prevent the sauce from seeping into the crust and making it soggy. Sprinkle on the remaining mozzarella.

Bake the pizza on the bottom rack of the oven for 18 to 20 minutes, until the cheese is bubbling and the bottom and edges of the crust are a rich golden brown (use a spatula to check the bottom). If the bottom is brown but the top still seems pale, transfer the pizza to the top rack and bake for 2 to 4 minutes longer. On the other hand, if the top seems fine but the bottom's not browned to your liking, leave the pizza on the bottom rack for another 2 to 4 minutes. Home ovens can vary a lot, so use the visual cues and your own preferences to gauge when you've achieved the perfect bake.

Remove the pizza from the oven and place the pan on a heatproof surface. Carefully run a table knife or spatula between the edge of the pizza and side of the pan to prevent the cheese from sticking as it cools. Let the pizza cool very briefly; as soon as you feel comfortable doing so, carefully transfer it from the pan to a cooling rack or cutting surface. This will prevent the crust from becoming soggy.

Serve the pizza anywhere from medium-hot to warm. Kitchen shears or a large pair of household scissors are both good tools for cutting this thick pizza into wedges.

Tips from our Bakers

Our base cheese of choice is a block of low-moisture mozzarella, coarsely grated. Want to experiment with different cheeses? Choose those that melt well: Fontina, cheddar, Jack, provolone, Gouda, and Muenster are all good candidates.

Want to add your own favorite toppings beyond red sauce and cheese? Vegetables or meats should be cooked before arranging them in a single layer atop cheese and sauce. Feel free to experiment with other sauces, too; pesto or white sauce are great alternatives to tomato. One hint: To avoid potential sogginess, stick to the same quantities and layering process for sauce and cheese listed above.

For an extra hit of flavor, sprinkle freshly grated hard cheese (e.g., Parmesan, Asiago, Romano) and/or fresh herbs (oregano, basil, thyme) over the hot pizza just before serving.

If you're serving the entire pizza (no leftovers) right away, you can serve it right from the pan if desired. We don't recommend using a knife to cut the pizza in the pan; it might mar your cast iron's surface. Instead, after loosening the edges, use a spatula to partially lift the pizza out of the pan, then cut a wedge using a pair of standard household scissors or kitchen shears. Remove the wedge and repeat until you've cut and served all of the pizza.

Feeding a larger group? Double all the ingredients in the recipe and follow the recipe instructions as written, dividing the dough into two pans (mix and match from the choices listed in step #6 above).
Want to make a gluten-free version of this recipe? Check out our [Gluten-Free Pan Pizza](#).

Gumbo

1 1/2 lbs fresh okra
1/2 lb. Andouille sausage
1/2 lb white chicken
1 1/2 lb raw shrimp with
14 oz diced tomatoes
1 onion
2 stalks celery
3 cloves garlic
½ + 2 tbs oil
½ cup flour
1 green pepper
1/4 tsp black pepper
1 tsp thyme
1 to 3 tsp salt
2 bay leaves
1/4 tsp cayenne pepper
2 tbs Creole seasoning
2 quarts boiling water for shrimp parts

Cut and fry Okra in 2 tbs oil until tender.

Devein shrimp and boil shells and heads in water until reduced by half.

Old-Fashioned Chicken and Dumplings

Prep Time: 1 hrs
Cook Time: 1 hrs 15 min
Yield: 6 servings

1 frying chicken (3 to 3 1/2 lbs.) cut up 1/2 tsp. pepper
1 large onion peeled, cut in half DUMPLINGS
1 large carrot peeled, cut in half 2 cups Martha White® Self-Rising Flour
1 large celery stalk cut in half 1/3 cup Crisco® All-Vegetable Shortening
8 cups water 1/3 stick OR Crisco® Baking Sticks All-Vegetable Shortening
2 tbsps. butter 1/2 cup chicken broth
1 tsp. salt

COMBINE chicken, onion, carrot, celery and water in Dutch oven. Bring to a boil. Reduce heat to low. Cover and simmer 1 hour or until tender. Remove chicken from broth. Remove vegetables from broth and discard. Cool chicken and broth slightly. Remove chicken from bones. Cut into bite-sized pieces. Skim fat from surface of cooled broth. Bring broth to a boil.

Add butter, salt and pepper.

PLACE flour in medium bowl. Cut in shortening with pastry blender or 2 knives until mixture resembles coarse crumbs. Add 1/2 cup chicken broth. Stir with fork until dough leaves sides of bowl.

ROLLED DUMPLINGS: Roll out dough on lightly floured surface to 1/8-inch thickness. Cut dough into strips or small squares.

DROP DUMPLINGS: Press dough on lightly floured surface to 1/2-inch thickness. Pinch off dough in small pieces.

DROP dumplings 1 at a time into boiling broth. Reduce heat to low. Cover and simmer 15 minutes or until dumplings are firm. Gently stir once or twice during cooking to prevent dumplings from sticking together. Stir chicken pieces into dumpling mixture just before serving.

Papas Shrimp and Grits

1 lb raw shrimp peeled and deveined and tails removed
1/2 lb Adele's Andouille Sausage cut into small pieces
1/4 stick butter
1 cup cream
2 cloves garlic or equivalent
1/4 cup chopped mushrooms
Small amount of chopped onions
Tony Chacheres Cajun seasoning or equivalent
1tbs fresh cilantro (Kroger sells in salad section)

Cheese Grits
2 cups water
1/2 cup cream
1/2 cup old fashioned grits (Quaker old fashioned works great) 1 cup shredded cheddar cheese

Sauce
In a pan melt 1/4 stick butter, sauté onions, sausage, garlic, mushrooms and Cajun seasoning and cook for ten minutes, (Note: Use Cajun seasoning like salt), add cream and stir constantly with a whisk for ten minutes and set aside.

Grits
In a pan, bring water to a boil, add grits and butter stirring constantly until grits a smooth, cook rolling instructions on container. Stir in cream and cheese and stir until smooth.

Shrimp

Prepare shrimp either on stove top or grill (I like to add either Old Bay or Blackening seasoning) don't overcook 5 to 8 minutes

Add shrimp to cream sauce and pour over grits garnish with fresh cilantro and whatever else you want to make the recipe your own.

Pizza Dough

1 1/3 cup all-purpose bread flour
1 tsp salt
1 tsp baking powder
1 Tbs sugar

Mix dry ingredients in a bowl with a whisk.

Add olive oil and water. Mix until a ball is formed. Let it rest in the bowl 15 minutes.

Turn out on a dusted flat surface and shape into a pizza.

Weeknight Bolognese

2 tablespoons good olive oil, plus extra to cook the pasta
1 pound lean ground sirloin
4 teaspoons minced garlic (4 cloves)
1 tablespoon dried oregano
1¼ cups dry red wine, divided
1 (28-ounce) can crushed tomatoes, preferably San Marzano
2 tablespoons tomato paste
Kosher salt and freshly ground black pepper
3/4 pound dried pasta, such as orecchiette or small shells
1/4 teaspoon ground nutmeg
1/4 cup chopped fresh basil leaves, lightly packed
1/4 cup heavy cream
1/2 cup freshly grated Parmesan cheese, plus extra for serving

Heat 2 tablespoons of olive oil in a large (12-inch) skillet over medium-high heat. Add the ground sirloin and cook, crumbling the meat with a wooden spoon, for 5 to 7 minutes, until the meat has lost its pink color and has started to brown. Stir in the garlic, oregano, and red pepper flakes and cook for 1 more minute. Pour 1 cup of the wine into the skillet and stir to scrape up any browned bits. Add the tomatoes, tomato paste, 1 tablespoon salt, and 1½ teaspoons pepper, stirring until combined. Bring to a boil, lower the heat, and simmer for 10 minutes.

Meanwhile, bring a large pot of water to a boil, add a tablespoon of salt, a splash of oil, and the pasta, and cook according to the directions on the box. While the pasta cooks, finish the sauce. Add the nutmeg, basil, cream, and the remaining ¼ cup wine to the sauce and simmer for 8 to 10 minutes, stirring occasionally until thickened. When the pasta is cooked, drain and pour into a large serving bowl. Add the sauce and ½ cup Parmesan and toss well. Serve hot with Parmesan on the side.

Note to self:

Made this recipe on Oct 18, 2019 and turned out good. Red pepper in original recipe was too much so I removed it.

Dressings and Dips

Buffalo Chicken Dip

Ingredients
8 oz. cream cheese
1/2 cup Ranch dressing
1/2 cup Frank's Buffalo Wing Sauce (I used the original, but if you prefer it spicier, you can use the hot wing sauce)
1-2 cups shredded white cheese (I used mozzarella)
2 cups cooked, chopped chicken breast

Microwave the cream cheese for 1 minute to soften. Stir in remaining ingredients. Bake at 350 for 20 minutes. Serve with tortilla chips of choice.

Southern Slaw Dressing

1 cup Dukes Mayo
6 tablespoons honey
2 tablespoons apple cider vinegar
3 tablespoons Dijon mustard
3 tablespoons barbecue sauce

Blend and refrigerate 2 hours

Slaw
1 head cabbage
1/4 cup carrots
1/2 small onion
Salt and pepper to taste

Shred with food processor. Place in colander and drain for two hours until all water is gone

Southern way to serve is to serve slaw and add dressing at table. Can be premixed and liquid drained before serving.

Meats

Mongolian Beef

1 1/4 lbs flank steak thinly sliced
1/4 cup + 2 teaspoons cornstarch divided use
3 tablespoons vegetable oil
1 1/2 teaspoons minced garlic
1 teaspoon minced ginger
1 teaspoon toasted sesame oil
1/2 cup low sodium soy sauce
1/3 cup water
1/2 cup dark brown sugar
1/2 cup green onions cut into 1-inch pieces
Salt and Pepper to taste

Place the flank steak and 1/4 cup cornstarch in a resealable plastic bag, shake to coat evenly.

Heat the vegetable oil in a large pan over high heat. Add the meat in a single layer and season to taste with salt and pepper (keeping in mind the sauce has plenty of salt in it!). Cook for 3-4 minutes per side or until browned. Cook in multiple batches if needed.

Remove the meat from the pan and place on a plate lined with paper towels.

Add the garlic and ginger to the pan and cook for 30 seconds. Add the soy sauce, sesame oil, water and brown sugar to the pan and bring to a simmer.

Mix the 2 teaspoons of cornstarch with 1 tablespoon of cold water. Add the cornstarch to the sauce and bring to a boil; boil for 30-60 seconds until just thickened.

Add the meat and green onions to the pan and toss to coat with the sauce. Serve over rice if desired.

Peppered Beef with Onion

1 pound beef tenderloin
1/4 teaspoon salt
1/4 teaspoon ground black pepper
1 large egg white, lightly beaten
2 tablespoons cornstarch
5 tablespoons vegetable oil - divided use
2 slices fresh ginger root
1 teaspoon Szechuan peppercorns
2 onions, thinly sliced
2 tablespoons dark soy sauce
1 1/2 teaspoons granulated sugar

Cut beef into thin slices 2 x 1 1/2-inches in size. Sprinkle with salt and a generous amount of pepper. Dip into egg white and dust with cornstarch.

Heat 4 tablespoons (1/4 cup) of the oil in a wok or frying pan over medium heat. When hot, add ginger and peppercorns. Stir-fry for 45 seconds. Add beef, spreading it out over the surface of the pan, and stir-fry for 1 minute over high heat.

Remove and set aside.

Add remaining 1 tablespoon oil to heat. Add onion and stir-fry for 1 1/2 minutes. Stir in soy sauce and sugar. Return beef and continue to stir-fry for 1 1/2 minutes over high heat. Serve with rice.

Makes 5 servings.

Perfect Prime Rib

Prep Time: 12 hours 15 mins
Cook Time: 5 hours 30 mins
Yield: 6 servings

1 3-rib bone-in Prime rib roast (about 6½ to 7 pounds)
2 tablespoons olive oil
2 tablespoons kosher salt
1 tablespoon freshly ground black pepper
5 pounds beef bones including meat and fat, such as necks, chuck bones, etc. I found neck bones on sale as well as some fatty rib pieces
1 ½ teaspoons kosher salt
½ teaspoon freshly ground black pepper
2 tablespoons olive oil
6 large garlic cloves, peeled and smashed
1/3 cup red wine such as merlot
2 cups water
2 tablespoons Worcestershire sauce
½ teaspoon gravy color and seasoning sauce such as Kitchen Bouquette

Place the beef on a platter and coat with oil, salt and pepper and refrigerate uncovered overnight fat side up. Five hours before serving, heat the oven to 450 degrees F.

Pull roast from refrigeration and let sit at room temperature while you roast the bones and fat.

In roasting pan place beef bones and fat, salt, pepper and oil and roast 30 minutes. Turn the bones and fat and roast 30 more minutes.

Reduce the oven to 250 degrees F and leave oven door open so the oven cools down to this new setting.

Remove pan from oven and place the garlic over the top of the bones then place the roast over that, fat side up.

Insert a probe thermometer into the fattest part of the roast and set alarm temperature to 125 degrees F for medium rare.

Our 6 ¼ pound roast took exactly 3½ hours to cook to an internal temperature of 125 degrees F. It will continue to cook outside of the oven to the proper medium rare doneness.

Remove beef to a platter and cover loosely with foil for 20 minutes to rest, no less.

Increase oven temperature to 450 degrees F. Place roasting pan with bones on stove top and add wine to deglaze.

When wine has almost evaporated, add water, Worcestershire sauce and gravy color and simmer until liquid has reduced to about a cup to a cup and a half. Strain out solids and pour Au Jus into sauce pan to heat when needed. After the roast has rested for 20 minutes, remove probe and place roast back on roasting pan and into hot oven and brown for 15-20 minutes or until desired crispiness.

Remove from oven, let sit five more minutes and carve.

Heat Au Jus to hot and serve on the side or over the slices. Serve Horseradish sauce on the side.

With a three-bone rib roast, three slices will have meat only and three will have bone in.

One last note; your roast may or may not have the end of the rib bones protruding out of the end. Either way, no change to cooking method, just wanted to point out that it is sold both ways.

Slow Cooked Salisbury Steak

Served with mashed potatoes and peas
Prep Time: 8-10 minutes
Cook Time: 6-8 hours
Servings: 4-6 people

Prep
4-6 whole formed hamburger patties 93/7 or leaner
1 T steak seasoning
1 1/2 C frozen chopped onion
1 pkg sliced mushrooms optional
1/4 C whole wheat flour
1 1/2 C beef broth

Add last 3 ingredients to medium container with lid.

Spray slow cooker with nonstick spray. Add meat patties and mushrooms if using. Layer if needed.

Shake broth mixture well and pour over meat patties. Cook on low for 6 - 8 hours. Meat will be pink inside which is normal. They will be done. Check with a meat thermometer to be sure.

Cook potatoes according to package directions and serve with green salad.

Salt and pepper to taste.

On Cooking Day
6 C salad greens
1 bag frozen mashed potato steamer

Salsa, Sauces, Seasonings, & Sides

Bill Knapp's Coleslaw

1 1/2 cups salad dressing (not mayonnaise)
1 tbsp plus 1/2 tsp prepared mustard
Pinch of salt
1 tbsp plus 1 tsp granulated sugar
1 1/2 lbs finely shredded green cabbage
3/4 cup chopped carrots
3 tbsp chopped onions

Blend together salad dressing, mustard, salt and sugar thoroughly with wire whip and refrigerate until ready to add to salad. Pour dressing over vegetables and mix until creamy and evenly blended. Refrigerate until served. Makes 8 servings.

Cajun Cream Sauce

4 tbs butter
4 cloves garlic minced
1/4 cup chopped onion
2 tbs olive oil
1/4 cup all-purpose flour
3 cups half and half
1/4 cup chopped mushrooms
1/4 cup Parmesan cheese
Blackening Seasoning to taste (Tony Chachere's - use like salt)
Pepper to taste

In a large saucepan melt butter and olive oil, add garlic, onions and cook until garlic is toasted and onion is clear. Add flour and seasoning cook until a dark brown rue is made. Add cream and cheese and bring to a boil. Simmer for 15 minutes season to taste.

Cajun Seasoning

2 tablespoons garlic powder
2 tablespoons <u>Italian seasoning</u>
2 tablespoons paprika
2 tablespoons Salt
1 tablespoon black pepper
1 tablespoon cayenne pepper
1 tablespoon dried thyme
1 tablespoon onion powder

Cucumber Sauce

Servings: 12
Yield: 3 1/2 Cups
Units: US

3 cups Greek yogurt (also called Yogurt Cheese, see below for alternative)
3 tablespoons lemon juice (or juice of one lemon)
1 garlic clove, minced
1 large English cucumber, diced (the long, skinny ones)
1 tablespoon salt (for salting cucumbers)
1 tablespoon fresh dill (or both, depending on preference) or 1 tablespoon of Fresh mint, chopped (or both, depending on preference)
Salt & freshly ground black

Peel cucumbers and dice. Put them in a colander and sprinkle with the tablespoon of salt (draws water out). Cover with a plate and sit something heavy on top. Let sit for 30-minute. Drain well and wipe dry with a paper towel. In food processor or blender, add cucumbers, garlic, lemon juice, dill and/or mint, and a few grinds of black pepper. Process until well blended, then stir into yogurt. Taste before adding any extra salt, then salt if needed. Place in refrigerator for at least two hours before serving so flavors can blend.

This will keep for a few days in the refrigerator, but you will need to drain off any water and stir each time you use it.

** If you can't find the thicker Greek Yogurt Cheese, you can use regular, plain yogurt that is either full fat or low fat. To thicken, spoon yogurt into cheese cloth that has been quadrupled. Draw the corners of the cloth up and tie together. Suspend above a bowl for 2 hours so that water can drip out. The consistency of the yogurt should be like that of sour cream.

You can skip this draining process, if you want, but you will have a moderately messier, runnier result.

Italian Seasoning

2 tablespoons dried basil
2 tablespoons dried oregano
2 tablespoons dried rosemary
2 tablespoons dried thyme
2 tablespoons dried marjoram

Peach Salsa

4 cups diced tomatoes
2 lg diced jalapeño peppers or whatever you have 1 lg ripe peach skinned and diced
1/4 cup chopped onion
2 cloves crushed garlic
1/4 cup sugar or sweetener
Crushed Cilantro to taste
Salt and pepper

Place all ingredients in a saucepan except cilantro and bring to a boil cook one minute and let rest. Add cilantro and process in a blender until smooth. Cool and serve. Add or subtract to your taste.

Peanut Sauce
3/23/2017

1/4 cup soy sauce
1/2 cup brown sugar
1/2 cup water
1/4 cup peanut butter
1 tsp onion powder
1/8 tsp black pepper
1 tsp garlic powder
½ tsp red pepper
1/8 tsp sesame oil

Blend in a saucepan and bring to a boil stirring intermittently. Serve over rice or steamed or wok-ed veggies.

Red Lobster Tartar Sauce

Yield: 1 cup
Units: US | Metric

1/3 cup Miracle Whip
2 tablespoons sweet pickle relish
1/4 cup powdered confectioners' sugar
3 tablespoons finely diced sweet white onions
3 teaspoons minced fresh carrots
2/3 cup fresh sour cream
¼ teaspoon fine ground table salt

Place onion in food processor; chop; transfer to small bowl; set aside.

Place carrot in food processor; chop; add to onion.

Combine remaining ingredients in separate bowl; whisk well to combine. Add onion and carrot; mix well. Cover; refrigerate at least 2 hours to allow flavors to meld.

Read more at: http://www.food.com/recipe/red-lobster-tartar-sauce-441074?oc=linkback

Tartar Sauce
Red Lobster Style

1/2 cup mayonnaise.
1 1/2 tablespoons white onions chopped.
1 tablespoon carrot finely diced.
1 tablespoon pickle relish do not use dill relish.
1 1/2 teaspoon sugar

Soups

Larry's Corn Chowder

6 strips bacon
1/4 stick butter
I medium onion chopped
1 cup chopped celery
1/2 cup chopped carrots
2 tablespoons old bay seasoning
1 Can cream style corn
4 links mild Italian sausage
1 box chicken stock
4 ears fresh corn cut and scraped
10 small red potatoes diced with skin on
Large container heavy whipping cream
Salt pepper to taste

Start with frying Italian sausage in a skillet and drain and set aside.

In a stock pot fry bacon and remove leaving grease.

Add butter, onion, celery and carrot and cook until tender, return sausage

and cream style corn, add chicken stock and old bay.

Cut and scrape corn add to pot

Dice potatoes and add to pot cook for 15 minutes over low heat.

Add cream and simmer until potatoes are tender

Crumble bacon you removed earlier and return to pot. Enjoy.

Larry's Corn Chowder – 2

1 stick butter
1 large onion diced
2 cups chopped celery
1 cup diced carrots
1/3 cup all-purpose flour
1 box chicken stock
1 can condensed milk
1 quart half and half
1 tbs old bay seasoning
1 can creamed corn
1 can yellow whole kernel corn
1 can white whole kernel corn
6 large, diced potatoes
Salt and pepper to taste

Place butter, onions, celery and carrots in large stock pot cook over medium heat until onions are clear. Add flour and brown for five minutes stirring frequently add chicken stock and bring to a boil.

Once boiling add corn, old bay, and condensed milk. Salt and pepper to taste and allow to simmer several minutes, then add half and half and bring to a boil. Place the diced potatoes in chowder and cook until potatoes are soft but still firm, let simmer on low heat for thirty minutes and serve.

Serving suggestion, place chopped green onion and bacon pieces in center of bowl.

Potato Chowder

1 stick butter
1/2 chopped onion
1 cup chopped celery
1/2 cup chopped carrots
1 can evaporated milk + 2 cups milk
1 can whole kernel corn
1 can cream style corn
3 cup diced red potatoes with skin on
Salt and pepper to taste

In a medium pan add butter, onion, celery, carrots, salt and pepper. cook until veggies are tender, add both corns and cook 10 minutes. Add both milks and bring to a boil.

Add potatoes and cook 15 more minutes. Put soup in a crock pot and cook on low for two more hours and serve.

Variations
Clams and juice, Italian sausage and old bay seasoning. Chicken stock and bacon bits are also good addition.

Red Beans and Rice Recipe

2 tablespoons vegetable oil or bacon drippings
1 cup chopped onions
1/2 cup chopped bell peppers
1/2 cup chopped celery
1 teaspoon salt
1/2 teaspoon cayenne pepper
1/4 teaspoon freshly ground black pepper
1 teaspoon dried thyme
2 bay leaves
1 pound boiled or baked ham cut, into 1/2-inch cubes
6 ounces smoked sausage, cut crosswise into 1/4-inch slices
1 pound dried red beans, rinsed and sorted through, soaked overnight and drained
3 tablespoons chopped garlic
8 to 10 cups water
Cooked white rice

Heat the oil/drippings in a large saucepan over medium high heat. Sauté the onions, bell peppers, celery, salt, cayenne, black pepper and thyme for about 5 minutes. Add the bay leaves, ham and sausage and sauté for 5 to 6 minutes. Add the beans, garlic, and enough water to cover the contents in the pot. Bring to a boil, reduce the heat to medium, and simmer uncovered, stirring occasionally for about 2 hours. Add more water if the mixture becomes dry and thick. Mash about half of the mixture against the side of the pot with a wooden spoon to add thickness. Continue to cook, stirring occasionally, for about 1 1/2 hours. The mixture should be creamy and the beans soft. Add more water if it becomes too thick. The finished product should be soupy, not watery. Remove the bay leaves and serve over cooked white rice.

Serve as a main dish or add grilled sausage or a piece of fried chicken on the side to round out the meal.

Red Beans and Rice

1 lb dry small red beans
1 1/2 to 2 lbs meaty ham shanks
4 cups water
4 cloves garlic, minced
1 large onion, chopped (about 2 cups)
1 1/2 cups chopped celery
1 cup chopped green bell pepper
1 Tbsp Worcestershire sauce
2 teaspoons of Cajun or Creole seasoning (Tony Chachere's or Zatarain's) or to taste*
Tabasco sauce**
Salt and pepper to taste
Cooked white rice (from about 3 cups raw rice)

*If you don't have access to packaged seasoning, just skip it and add some thyme (fresh or dried), a bay leaf (in with the beans and shanks in step 2), and a little paprika
**We used a combo of Chipotle Tabasco sauce and regular Tabasco, could also use cayenne pepper

Soak the beans: Place dried beans in a large bowl and cover them with cold water by a couple of inches. Let soak for 8 hours or overnight. (You can quick soak them by putting them in a bowl and pouring boiling water over them, covering them by 2 inches, then letting them soak for two hours.) Drain.

Cook beans with ham, garlic, onion, water: Place beans, ham shanks, garlic, chopped onion, and water in a large (8-quart) pot and bring to a boil. Reduce to a simmer and cover, simmer for 1 1/2 hours or until beans are tender.
Remove ham shanks, separate meat from bones: Remove ham shanks from the pot to a dish. Let cool slightly then shred the meat away from the bones. Return the meat back to the pot.

Add vegetables, seasonings, cook until thick: Add the celery, bell peppers, Worcestershire and seasonings. Cover and cook for another hour or until the mixture gets thick.

Season to taste with Tabasco sauce, salt and pepper.

Serve over rice.

Shrimp and Crab Bisque

3 tablespoons butter
2 tablespoons chopped green onion
2 tablespoons chopped celery
3 tablespoons all-purpose flour
2 1/2 cups milk
1/2 teaspoon freshly ground black pepper
1 tablespoon tomato paste
1 cup heavy whipping cream
8 ounces crab meat
4 to 8 ounces small, cooked shrimp or other seafood
2 tablespoon sherry wine

Melt the butter in a Dutch oven or large saucepan over medium-low heat; add the chopped green onion and celery. Sauté, stirring, until tender.

Blend the flour into the butter and vegetables until well incorporated. Continue cooking, stirring, for about 2 minutes.

Warm the milk in another saucepan over medium heat.

Slowly stir in the warmed milk and continue cooking and stirring until thickened.

Add the freshly ground black pepper, tomato paste, and heavy cream.

If desired, puree the soup in a blender or food processor** at this point and then return it to the saucepan. Stir in the crab, shrimp, and the sherry. Bring to a simmer.

Tips and Variations
Feel free to add small, cooked bay scallops or lobster instead of the shrimp.

Replace the green onions with finely chopped shallots.

If desired, garnish the soup with thinly sliced green onion tops, cilantro, or parsley. Or add a spoonful of sour cream and swirl it.

Slow Cooker Creamy Tortellini Soup
Author Karina - Cafe Delites

Slow Cooker Creamy Tortellini Soup is pure comfort food, loaded with vegetables, Italian sausage and cheese tortellini! NO flour and NO heavy cream!

Servings 10

500 grams | 1 pound ground Italian sausage (or ground chicken, turkey or beef), browned*
1 brown onion, chopped
2 large carrots, chopped
2 stalks celery, chopped
4 cloves garlic, minced
1 tablespoon Italian seasoning
2 teaspoon beef bouillon powder (or chicken)
1/2 teaspoon salt
4 cups beef broth (or chicken or vegetable broth -- I use low sodium)
1/4 cup cornstarch mixed and dissolved in 1/4 cup water
3 x 340 gram | 12-ounce cans full fat evaporated milk or half and half
1 x 340 gram | 12 ounce packet three cheese tortellini (I used dried not fresh; choose any flavour you like)
5 cups fresh baby spinach
1 cup milk

Place the browned sausage, onion, carrots, celery, garlic, Italian seasoning, beef bouillon powder, salt, and broth in a 6-quart / litre slow cooker bowl. Cover and cook on high for 4 hours or low for 7 hours.

Uncover and skim any fat that is sitting on the top of the soup with a spoon; discard. Stir in the cornstarch mixture with the evaporated milk (or half and half or cream). Add the tortellini and mix well. Cover again and cook on HIGH heat setting for a further 45 minutes until the soup has thickened, and the tortellini is soft and cooked through.

Add in the spinach, pressing the leaves down to completely submerse into the liquid. Cover again for a further 5-10 minutes until the leaves have wilted.

Pour in milk in 1/3 cup increments, as needed, to reach your desired thickness and consistency (I needed 1 cup); taste test and season with extra salt ONLY if needed, and pepper to suit your tastes.
Serve with crusty warmed bread

Recipe Notes
*Italian sausage gives this soup an amazing flavour, but you can substitute it with ground chicken, turkey or beef sausage. OR use plain ground meats if you don't like sausage. For vegetarian options, leave the meat out altogether.

The soup thickens as it cools and absorbs quite a lot of liquid. Extra milk may be needed when reheating leftovers to reach your desired level of creaminess.

www.ingramcontent.com/pod-product-compliance
Lightning Source LLC
Chambersburg PA
CBHW030447100526
44580CB00001B/18